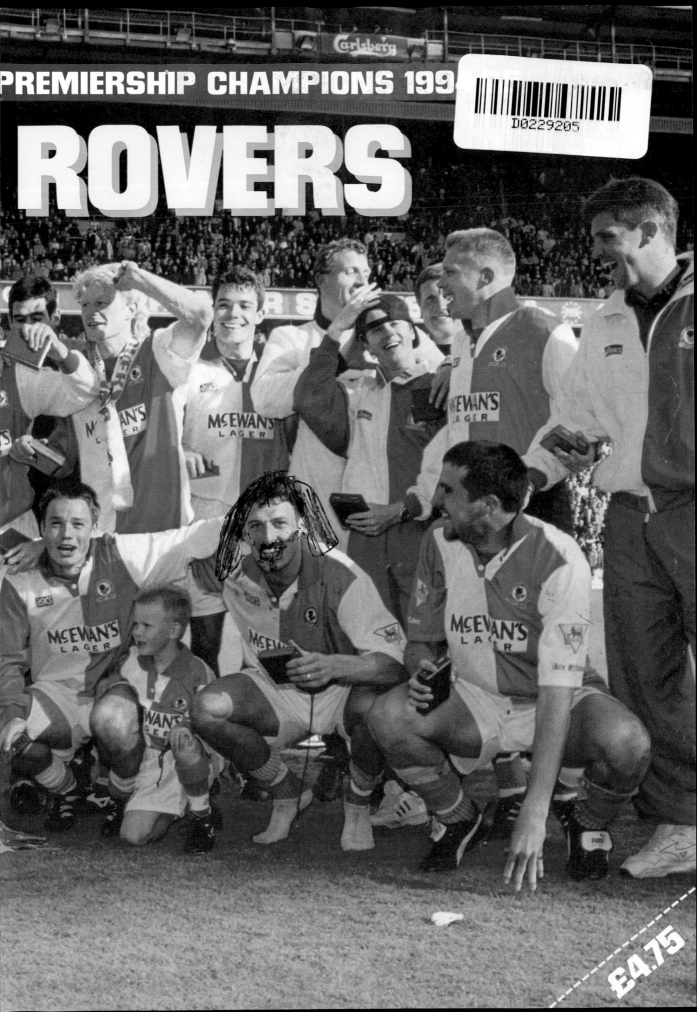

PREMIERSHIP CHAMPIONS 199...

ROVERS

£4.75

THE FIRING SQUAD

HOW would you like to stand between the sticks when Ian Wright is taking a penalty or Stuart Pearce is lining up one of his devastating free-kicks. Our top 'keepers are facing that sort of firing squad every week, but who are the sharp shooters they least like to face? We asked some of them.

Top stoppers reveal the master marksmen

TONY COTON (ManCity): "My old team-mate Niall Quinn takes some beating. He is brilliant in the air and he can also cause you a lot of trouble on the ground. He is not just a great scorer, but also a terrific goal-maker. As far as the rest are concerned you can never take your eyes off Mark Hughes. How often he grabs a goal out of nothing. But I believe the best for me has to be **Ian Rush**. He is totally instinctive and they are the worst strikers to face. He doesn't stop to think as he doesn't have to - he just reacts."

BRYAN GUNN (Norwich): "I have played against most of the top guns of today and I don't think there is anyone with the finishing ability of **Chris Sutton.** He could be devastating just in training so when he is playing he has even more of an edge. There are a lot of great strikers about but he is the tops."

DAVID SEAMAN (Arsenal): "Until he retired, I would always have named **Gary Lineker** as the worst striker to face - he always seemed to put one past me. But there are so many great strikers about at the moment that is very difficult to pick one as the best. Alan Shearer, especially with Chris Sutton, can be highly dangerous. Ian Wright is lethal - fortunately I only have to face him in training. Mark Hughes is always a threat and Ian Rush can be a nightmare. Liverpool have another danger now in Robbie Fowler. I wouldn't want to play him every week."

NEVILLE SOUTHALL (Everton): "No striker is anything less than dangerous - otherwise they wouldn't be doing their job. I could list a lot of them who I would rather not be playing against but for me I have to say that over the years the most consistently dangerous forward in the country is my Welsh team-mate **Ian Rush.** His record speaks for itself and I think he should have been banned a long time ago! He gets far too many great goals."

PETER SCHMEICHEL (Man United): "I believe that we have some of the most dangerous strikers in the business, especially since **Andy Cole** joined us at the start of the year. I would have named him even before he joined United. He is very fast, very strong and has all the abilities of a natural goalscorer. You cannot forget Alan Shearer or Jurgen Klinsmann when you are talking about great strikers, and Matthew Le Tissier is also one to watch - very dangerous."

MARK CROSSLEY (Nottingham Forest): "There are several I have to watch. Robbie Fowler is a real livewire in the box - just like Ian Rush. Ian Wright is devastating and he often seems to put one past me. He's done it with both Palace and Arsenal. I have seen enough of Stan Collymore to know that I prefer him on our side. Chris Sutton is very powerful, very good in the air and has a real eye for goal - quite frightening really. But the top all-rounder for me is **Alan Shearer.** He is probably the most complete player in the game."

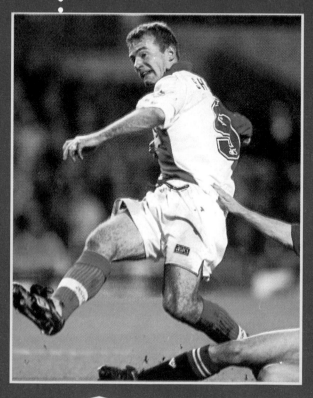

Now turn over the page for more 'keeper capers

THE FIRING SQUAD

ANDY GORAM
(Rangers):
"Not all the great strikers are in England. Mark Hateley is a terrific goalscorer and I can't understand why he was not been called back into the England squad. Ally McCoist is far from finished. Anyone who scores as many goals as he has simply has to be one of the most dangerous men around. **John Collins,** of Celtic packs a really hard shot and there's Duncan Shearer, Tommy Coyne, Billy Dodds, John Robertson and many others. When you start to list them you realise just how much fire power there is in the Premier League in Scotland - and there's a lot in the lower divisions too."

PAT BONNER:
(Celtic)
"I wouldn't want to be on the receiving end of a John Collins shot - they go like a rocket. Playing for the Republic of Ireland has meant that I have faced some tough opponents but they don't come much more deadly than people like Ally McCoist and Mark Hateley - they are both very dangerous . Duncan Ferguson is also a lethal player. It is very difficult to pick one but I would probably go for **Brian Laudrup** - he has it all."

CHRIS WOODS:
(Sheff. Wed)
"Britain has always produced great strikers and I don't think they come any more dangerous than **Alan Shearer.** He will help make goals for others but he is at his best in the box going for goal himself. He is very powerful and skilful and has all the courage it takes to turn half-chances into goals. Alan uses his strength very well and he has great balance, as well as an instinct for scoring. I am sure he will become one of the all-time great English strikers."

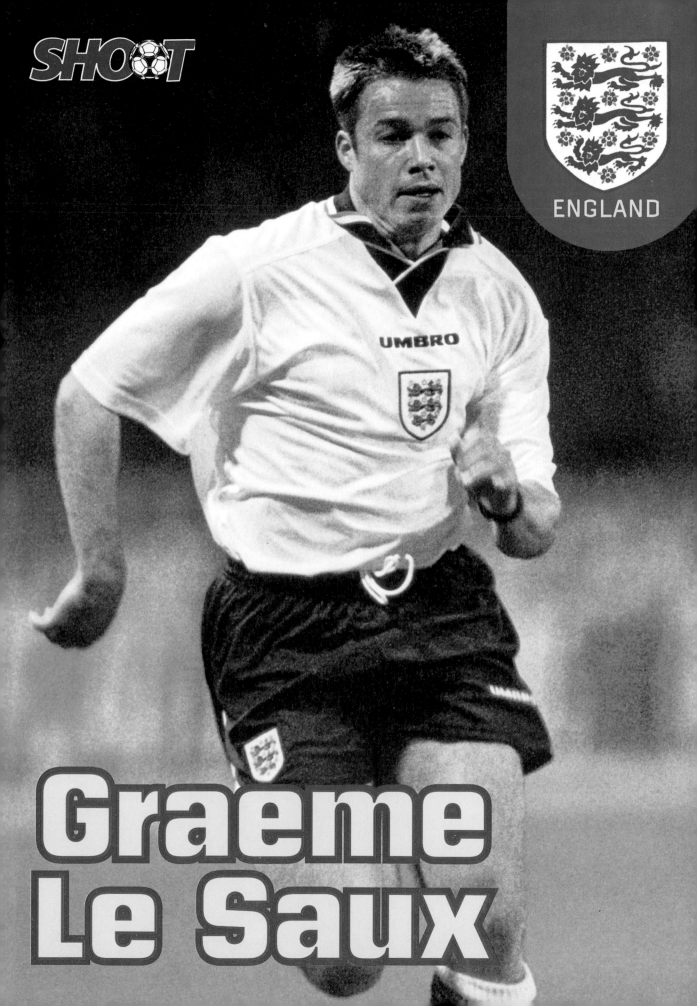

SHOOT

ENGLAND

Graeme Le Saux

Shaggy Mark I: Darren Anderton

THE PLAYERS......

JUST AS every club has a nickname, most players are often given a different tag...and it's not always complimentary.

At least two star Premiership players have been nicknamed "SHAGGY" by their so-called mates and both for the same reason. **DARREN ANDERTON** and **STEVE McMANAMAN** of Liverpool both carry that nickname because their team-mates reckon they have no dress sense and can actually be scruffy. They're both pretty neat on the pitch though.

There are also a couple of "TRIGGERS" after the character in TV's Only Fools And Horses. **ROB JONES** of Liverpool is one of them as Ian Rush explained: "We call Rob that because he is a bit slow on the uptake." Portsmouth's **GERRY CREANEY** was also given that tag when he was with Celtic. "It's the way he smiles after getting a goal - he looks just like him," said former team-mate Peter Collins.

Newcastle's **BARRY VENISON** is almost proud of his nickname.

"The lads have been calling me JON BON JOVI. We've played his video on the coach a lot and they reckon I look like him," said Barry.

Another Newcastle star with a strange nickname is **LEE CLARK**.

"They call me NASH. It's part of the Geordie language and it means I've got to go somewhere quickly. I used to use it a lot and it stuck to me," Lee explained.

JASON WILCOX is nicknamed WINDY because he played in the same position as a former Blackburn Rovers favourite - Ian "Windy" Miller. David May started to call Jason that and the name stuck.

How about this for a good one? Manchester City's **TERRY PHELAN** is called THE ANGRY ANT! Why? Let Niall Quinn explain: "It's because he is small and always has a grimace on his face. He never actually gets angry but he always looks like he is just about to."

Queens Park Ranges 'keeper **TONY ROBERTS** (centre picture) has his mum to thank for the nickname that has stuck with him.

"I used to jump and dive about the

The Angry Ant: Terry Phelan

Shaggy Mark II: Steve McManaman

WHAT'S IN A NICKNAME?

goal like a frog when I was at school and everyone started to call me FROGGIT. I thought I had left all that behind then my mum mentioned it to a group of fans and now it's back again."

Here are a few other nicknames of the soccer stars:-

SCOT GEMMILL (Nottingham Forest) - Pip
SOL CAMPBELL (Tottenham) - Soul Man
STUART PEARCE (Nottingham Forest) - Psycho (the original)
SCOTT OAKES (Luton) - Wonderboy
JUSTIN EDINBURGH (Tottenham) - Wing Nut

THE CLUBS

AND what about the clubs? It is obvious that 'Spurs' is a shortened version of Hotspur but where did Tottenham get that Hotspur bit from? The club was originally called Hotspur FC after the famous Harry Hotspur, an adventure hero whose real name was Henry Percy and was the son of the Duke of Northumberland.

Grimsby are known as The Mariners as the town from which they take their name was once one of Europe's busiest fishing ports. The fishing has lessened but the port is still going strong so they are still on the crest of a wave.

Bristol Rovers are called The Pirates because many of the real pirates of old set sail from Bristol. But when Rovers first started they wore an all-black strip and were nicknamed the Black Arabs.

Walsall's nickname of The Saddlers comes from the leatherworkers who were involved in the club when it started back in 1888. The same applies to Northampton which is still the hub of the shoe-making industry in Britain. Northampton have been known as The Cobblers since they were formed in 1897, which is a little strange because at the beginning they were actually a team of schoolteachers.

Wycombe are known as The Chairboys because furniture making has always been a busy local industry and in total contrast, Lincoln City have been known as The Imps throughout their history because of a local legend.

Derby County was formed by Derbyshire County Cricket club but instead of being called The Bats, they became The Rams because of the local connection with sheep farming.

Luton are known as The Hatters because of the local trade just as Scunthorpe are called The Iron for the same reason, iron and steel being major industries in the area.

The list is endless with some of the most spectacular nicknames being in Scotland where it is not uncommon for the Red Lichties (Arbroath) to face the Gable Endies (Montrose).

At least now if someone mentions The Hatters' Wonderboy you might have some idea who they are talking about!

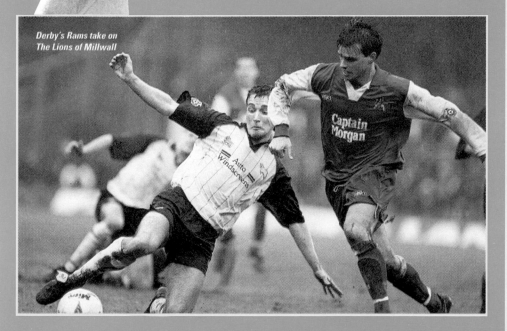

Derby's Rams take on The Lions of Millwall

Has football gone mad, or what?

Game for a laugh!

GRIMSBY TOWN used to show a nice gesture to visiting teams by presenting them with a huge box of fish to take home. The opposition appreciated the kindness of The Mariners although a few were not too sure. For instance, if you were Plymouth or Torquay or perhaps Swansea, it was a long coach journey home with the fish getting warmer and warmer. Bet it taught players to keep their 'plaice'.

WHAT do West Ham and Swansea have in common? Well, both Upton Park and Vetch Field used to be fields growing vegetables. Could be useful if the ref ever loses the pea out of his whistle!

NOTTINGHAM FOREST was founded by a men's hockey team back in 1865. Of course, they needed some kit so they bought some - a set of red caps! They did wear their hockey gear as well though, otherwise they might have been arrested!

REFEREES aren't as daft as some people suppose. When a Scottish manager had an injury crisis leading up to an important Cup-tie he hoped the ref would call the game off because of a heavy frost. The ref inspected the pitch the evening before the game and said it would be playable the next day. Not to be outdone, the crafty manager had the pitch watered so that it would freeze. The ref made another inspection and had no alternative but to cancel the game. But then he checked with the Met office, discovered that there had been no rain and the manager was caught out. Needless to say he got into hot water!

FOOTBALLERS love to play practical jokes on one another. David Bardsley at QPR is one of the worst for catching his team-mates. But one day they got their own back. They grabbed him while he was taking a shower and put a ball and chain on him so that he couldn't move. Then they all went out for a drink. An hour and a half later they came back and David was still there. He has gradually been gaining revenge ever since.

HOWARD McGARVEY was once stretchered off during a Scotland-Italy international at Ibrox - and he wasn't even playing! Italian star Alberto Di Chiari was being stretchered off by two ambulancemen - one of them was Howard. Unfortunately, Howard slipped and damaged his own ankle so badly that he also had to be stretchered off. The fans howled with laughter at the Laurel and Hardy capers going on in front of them. Howard laughs now but it was a bit more painful - and embarrassing - at the time.

WHEN Colin Murphy was manager of Lincoln City he got fed up with telling the directors that he needed more players. To prove his point he once picked his reserve goalkeeper to play in the first team - as striker!

RANGERS star Brian Laudrup is an expert on wines and runs an import business with his brother Michael. Imagine then how they would react to Everton and Wales goalkeeper Neville Southall's favourite drink. When asked, he said: "I prefer a nice cup of tea."

YOU CAN tell something about footballers by what they have on their answerphone messages. If you call Sheffield Wednesday's Chris Bart-Williams you will get your ears bashed by loud rap music. If you phone Derby's USA international John Harkes you might think you have got another famous name because John likes to do impersonations of showbiz stars. He leaves messages in different voice on his answerphone and keeps changing them to amuse and entertain callers.

Game for a laugh!

LIVERPOOL tough guy Neil Ruddock can't complain when people suggest he damaged his head when he was a boy - he did! He banged his forehead and had to have stitches. Then on the way back to hospital to have them removed he hit the back of his head and had to have stitches there. He must have more scars than Frankenstein's monster!

ALAN SHEARER will willingly tell you about his liking for chicken and beans before a match, but the Blackburn and England star will probably not tell you that he was nicknamed "Smokey" for a while. Why? Because he had a passion for Smokey Bacon crisps. Wonder if he prefers Walker's?

WYCOMBE WANDERERS manager Martin O'Neill has dozens of stories to tell about his former Nottingham Forest boss Brian Clough. One of his favourites is the team talk. "Sometimes the boss would get us together on a Friday, sit us down, pour a lager and eventually start the team talk by asking, "Who are we playing tomorrow'?"

THE NAME'S not always the same. Mark Hughes actually uses his second name. His real first name is Leslie. Would it sound the same if you heard commentators talking about Les Hughes of Manchester United? And what about his team-mate Ryan Giggs. His other name is Joseph and he was very nearly called that. Can you imagine hearing about the skills of Joe Giggs? And finally, what about Mark walters' lucky escape. The Liverpool star's middle name was nearly his first. What is it? EVERTON!

Game for a laugh!

SHOOT

John Moncur

WEST HAM UNITED F.C.

WEST HAM

SHOOT

Tottenham

Darren Anderton

TEL'S TALE

IF ENGLAND can win the European Championship in 1996, coach Terry Venables will be just one step away from becoming the most successful England boss of all time. Little did his school mates in Dagenham know that the lad they kicked about with in the playground in the post-war years would one day reach the top of the ladder in English soccer. Here's how he got there...

The wonder years

TEL was born in Dagenham on January 6th, 1943. His father, Fred, had been in the navy but took a job as a lorry driver to look after the family, but it was Tel's granddad who first encouraged him to start kicking a ball - a skill that became is favourite pastime.

At the age of 11, his career really began when he played for Lymington School. He was also into cricket and long distance running and represented his school at these sports too. But it was soccer that really grabbed him and he was soon playing for the Dagenham district schools side. He began training as a schoolboy with West Ham and achieved an ambition when he turned out for England schoolboys.

Venables was also a keen autograph hunter and would hang around London rail stations when he knew teams were arriving so he could get some signatures. But it was his own signature that was wanted in 1958 when he signed as an apprentice for Chelsea.

Star in the making

Terry did not sign professional forms at first because he wanted to play in the 1960 Olympic Games and indeed he did play for the

England amateur side. But at the age of 16 he made his senior debut for Chelsea in February 1960. When the Olympic squad was announced, Venables was not included and in August 1960 he became a full professional.

As his Chelsea career progressed, so did his international career. He played for the England youth team and then moved onto the Under-23 side. Meanwhile he was becoming a favourite at Stamford Bridge and during his time there, The Blues won promotion to the First Division, won the League Cup and competed in Europe.

Terry also won a full cap during his Chelsea days. He was picked to play against Belgium on October 21st, 1964 at Wembley. The match ended in a 2-2 draw. On December 9th of that year he won his second, and last cap, in a 1-1 draw against Holland in Amsterdam.

SHOOT plots the rise to stardom of the England supremo

On the move

Tottenham were not the first club to show an interest in Terry. Years before there had been a chance that he might join Manchester United. But when Spurs offered £60,000 for him in May 1966 it was to change his life.

At Spurs he became even more popular, presenting a cockney figure who impressed the White Hart Lane faithful. Probably his best moment was the 1967 FA Cup Final when he helped them beat his old club, Chelsea, 2-1 at Wembley. The Spurs team on that occasion contained quite a list of pedigree players who have made an indelible mark in soccer - Jennings, Kinnear, Knowles, Mullery, England, Mackay, Robertson, Greaves, Gilzean, Saul and, of course, Terry Venables.

After three years at Tottenham, Terry was on the move again. Queens Park Rangers bought him for £70,000 on June 5th, 1969 and he remained at Loftus Road for five years. During his spell he helped

QPR to win back their place in the top division and hold onto it.

It was time to move again in September 1974 but he remained in London, this time going to Crystal Palace with Ian Evans in a joint £70,000 deal. Palace wanted him mostly for his experience and he joined them as player-coach. Malcolm Allison was then manager at Selhurst Park.

Venables the boss

In June 1976, Venables finally stepped over the line and became manager of Palace. In his first season in charge - 1976/77 -the

club won promotion from the old Third Division. Two seasons later they won the Division Two Championship and were back among the big names of the game.

Almost retracing his steps, Venables resigned from Palace in October 1980 to return to Queens Park Rangers. In his second season he took them to Wembley where they were beaten in the 1982 FA Cup Final after a replay by, of all people, Tottenham - a Glenn Hoddle penalty deciding the match.

By the end of the 1982-83 season Venables had taken QPR back to the top as Champions of Division Two. With an eye for business, he also became a major shareholder and managing director of the club.

Tel's reign in Spain

A year passed and then came an offer he could not refuse - from Barcelona. Terry hit the headlines when he was appointed boss of the giant Spanish club in May 1984. He was eventually sacked three years later but in between he took them to the Spanish title and to the Final of the European Cup.

Venables was not out of work for long. His beloved Tottenham had parted company with David Pleat

and needed a new boss. Terry was available and, in October 1987, he was appointed. Under his guidance, Tottenham regained their momentum and went on to win the FA Cup in 1991, beating Nottingham Forest 2-1.

Terry never could resist getting involved in business. Since his teens he had shown an entrepreneurial streak and formed various companies. The opportunity to be involved in a Spurs takeover was too much of a temptation. He joined forces with Alan Sugar in a successful bid and became chief executive of the club.

Problems arose in the partnership and in June 1993, Terry was sacked amid a lot of acrimony. The newspapers were full of headlines and speculation for weeks.

England expects

Meanwhile, England were going from bad to worse in the World Cup qualifying matches and it seemed only a matter of time before manager Graham Taylor was on his way. That eventually happened of course and, in January 1994, Terry Venables became boss - or coach as the FA decided to call the job.

On March 8th, 1994 Wembley rang to the sound of 71,970 fans who turned up to show their support for England in their first game under Venables against Denmark. It was only a friendly but they were delighted with the 1-0 victory. Were England on the way to better days?

Venables has set about the England job in the same style as he has approached his other management appointments.

Whether he will still be in charge after 1996 remains to be seen.

A European win will mean yes, with the World Cup a very real target in 1998.

Then his story would be complete.

Andy Impey

goal

QPR v Arsenal

SHOOT

RUSH AND FOWLER fly the flag for Liverpool. They have linked brilliantly to capture a trophy for their side (the Coca-Cola Cup) and have Europe in their sights. When the Liverpool marksmen are in full flight no side is safe from their bombardment.

Salute the RAF

WORD FROM THE BOSS

"They are a terrific combination of experience and enthusiasm with skill and deadly scoring abilities as part of their ammunition." **ROY EVANS**

DID YOU KNOW?

- Ian was born on October 21st, 1961.
- Robbie was born on April 9th, 1975.
- When Rush began his Liverpool career in the 1981-82 season, Robbie was six-years-old.
- Ian has hit more Mersey derby goals than any other player, including four in the November 1982 clash.
- Robbie was Liverpool's top scorer last season - just ahead of Ian.
- Rush has won every domestic medal, Fowler has just started with the Coca-Cola Cup.
- Robbie scored after three minutes of his England Under-21 debut.
- Ian is Wales' top scorer of all-time.

Rush on Fowler

"Robbie is a natural goalscorer. He is not afraid to try things and that is important if you are going to score regularly."

Fowler on Rush

"Ian has been and still is one of my heroes. It is like playing alongside a legend."

DYNAMIC DUOS

No.1 Rush & Fowler

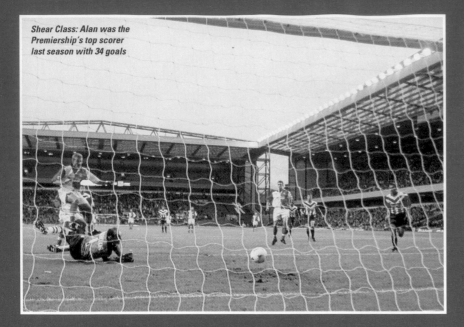

Shear Class: Alan was the Premiership's top scorer last season with 34 goals

CHRIS SUTTON and Alan Shearer did as much as anyone at Blackburn to bring the Premiership trophy to Ewood Park. Together they have combined to give goalkeepers the worst back-aches in the business, scoring more than half of Rovers' League goals last term.

Send for the SAS

DID YOU KNOW!

•Alan was born in Newcastle on August 13th, 1970.
•Chris was born in Nottingham on March 10th, 1973.
•Chris scored in his second ever senior game - and so did Alan.
•They have both captained the England Under-21 side.
•Both are keen cricketers.
•Alan was Britain's costliest player until Chris broke that record.
•Between them they scored more than 50 goals last season.
•They both made their senior debuts against London clubs.

WORD FROM THE BOSS

"They fitted in well together straight from the start. It was not an accident. They made their minds up from the start and have worked hard to achieve a good partnership."
KENNY DALGLISH

Shearer on Sutton

"We soon developed an understanding on the pitch, as well as a friendship off it. I always know I can rely on Chris."

Sutton on Shearer

"Since linking up with Alan at Blackburn, I have come to appreciate him all the more. He is a brilliant player and a great partner."

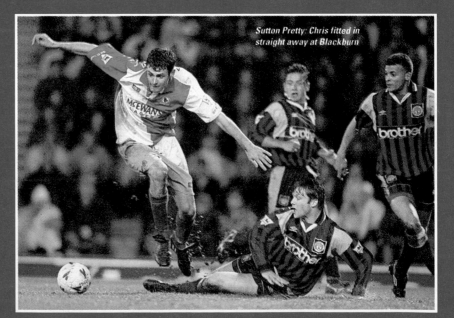

Sutton Pretty: Chris fitted in straight away at Blackburn

DYNAMIC DUOS

No.2 Sutton & Shearer

McCoist and Hateley are still the most potent force in Scotland. Injuries may have prevented them from breaking records last season but they are not finished yet. In recent years they have showed their killer instinct time and again to become the deadliest duo north of the border.

Ally Up. Every time McCoist scores he increases his all-time Premier record

Dial M for Goals

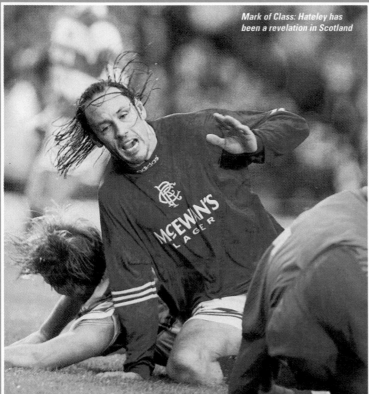

Mark of Class: Hateley has been a revelation in Scotland

DID YOU KNOW?
- Mark was born in Derby on November 7th, 1961.
- Ally was born in Bellshill, Glasgow on September 24th, 1962.
- Ally is the Scottish Premier's top scorer of all time and adds to his record every time he scores.
- Mark is probably the most popular Englishman in Scotland and is the only one to be made Scottish Footballer of the Year.
- Ally has twice been Europe's top League scorer.
- When Ally was injured, Mark became Rangers top scorer.
- Ally once sang with Wet Wet Wet.

WORD FROM THE BOSS
"They are two great footballers with the ability play to each other's strength. They both work hard but their partnership comes naturally. They are a tremendous pairing."
WALTER SMITH

Ally on Mark
"I love playing alongside Mark. His pace and power scares teams to death. He's great for me - a terrific partner who creates lots of chances for me and can put them away himself."

Mark on Ally
"Once Ally gets into the box there is no stopping him. He is a great team man and fun to be with but there is also the deadly streak of a great striker. When he is playing he means business."

DYNAMIC
DUOS

Spotlight on football's famous followers

YOU JUST never know who you are going to sit next to at a soccer match these days. Sometimes there are as many stars off the pitch as on it. Here are just a few of the famous names that you might see at a football ground any Saturday afternoon.

BOBBY DAVRO (Spurs)

Tottenham have their fair share of famous fans. Warren Mitchell - well-known as West Ham fan Alf Garnett - is really a Spurs fan, while mimic Bobby Davro is also a White Hart Lane regular.

"Things have really turned around at Tottenham. Their troubles are now behind them and we can look forward to winning some trophies. Signing Jurgen Klinsmann was a real masterstroke. He even made an impression on me!"

JIMMY CRICKET (Rochdale)

Rochdale even have a star supporter in Jimmy Cricket. The crazy comic lives on the edge of the town and is a keen fan.

"I would love to play for them. I went for a trial but they wouldn't let me play in my wellies. I said to the manager, "Come here '...what's wrong with my wellies? He said, 'You've got to play in boots'. So I took the ball to the chemists and they threw me out!"

ROD STEWART (Scotland)

Pop megastar Rod Stewart has a full-size soccer pitch in the grounds of his Essex home and Leeds United have been known to use it as a training pitch when they are playing in London. But Rod follows several clubs.

"Aberdeen is where I was born so I follow The Dons. Manchester United and Celtic are two of the greatest clubs in the world so I look out for them, and I also have a soft spot for Crewe.

"And I am a big Scotland fan of course. One of these years we are going to shock everyone - and win the World Cup!" Don't hold your breath, Rod!

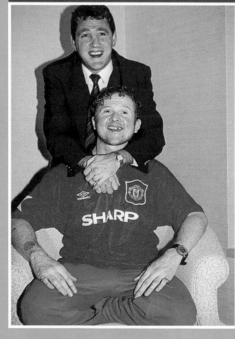

MICK HUCKNELL (Man Utd)

Lead singer Mick Hucknall is another pop star who likes his soccer. His favourites? Manchester United, of course.

"They are the best club in the world. I have supported United for as long as I can remember and the last few seasons in particular have been brilliant," says Mick. "I love the club, I love Old Trafford and I love their main colours." Wonder why?

FANS AIN'T WHAT

ROBBIE WILLIAMS (Port Vale)

Pop heart-throbs Take That are pretty strong Manchester United followers, except for Robbie Williams who is always keen to wave the flag for his beloved Port Vale.

"I've always followed them, they are a great club and have great fans," says Robbie. "Their history might not be as spectacular as some clubs but I'm confident that Vale have a great future. I shall go on supporting them whatever."

GRAHAM GOOCH (West Ham)

It is well-known that Prime Minister John Major and a number of other politicians are Chelsea fans, but did you know that, as well as Heartbeat star Nick Berry, West Ham have a star supporter in former England cricket captain Graham Gooch?

"The Hammers are my local side and I have followed them for years," he says. "I train with them as well. They work very hard. Tony Cottee is one of my favourite players but you can't help admiring Julian Dicks - he's a real tough defender."

NORMAN WISDOM (Newcastle)

Newcastle have an unlikely fan in Norman Wisdom, who used to be a Brighton director. "I still follow Brighton but because I have an old pal in Newcastle I spend a lot of time there and we hardly ever miss a chance to go and see Kevin Keegan's men - aren't they doing brilliantly?"

JIM BOWEN (Blackburn)

Champions Blackburn are double tops, according to Bullseye host Jim Bowen.

"If I can't get to a game I always tune in to the radio or the TV to keep up with what's going on. Even in my pre-showbiz days I was a Blackburn fan. I think they're super, smashing, lovely, great."

GARY GLITTER (Anyone)

Actor Tony Robinson can often be seen at Bristol City games, while Gary Glitter could turn up almost anywhere. "I move house a lot and follow whichever is my nearest club. The trouble is that I never actually stop supporting the clubs I have followed before, so I find myself watching out for Chelsea, Oxford, Bristol City, Bristol Rovers and Torquay!"

THEY USED TO BE!

BLACKBURN

ARTE ET LABORE

Blackburn Rovers are set to become a major force in English football.

The famous Ewood Park club was one of the most successful in the country in the late 1880s and were one of the founders members of the Football League in 1888.

They won the FA Cup five times between 1884 and 1891 and now, over one 100 years later, they are set for a return to those glory, glory days.

Their Premiership triumph last season was their first major trophy since 1928, but there's no way it will take them 67 years to win another one. Not with Jack Walker and Kenny Dalglish around.

Walker's millions and Dalglish's shrewd buying have turned Rovers from Second Division also-rans into Premiership Champions in just three years, and they haven't finished yet.

The club is determined to become even bigger and better and there's no doubt that the platform is there for them to do just that.

It is widely accepted that the first trophy is always the hardest to win and Blackburn broke through that barrier when they pipped Manchester United for the Premier crown last May - their first League title for 81 years!

And with the money available it won't be their last for 81 years.

Top Ten Transfers

PLAYER	FROM
Alan Shearer	Southampton
Chris Sutton	Norwich
Tim Flowers	Southampton
David Batty	Leeds
Tim Sherwood	Norwich
Graeme Le Saux	Chelsea
Noel Brotherston	Tottenham
Duncan McKenzie	Chelsea
Howard Kendall	Stoke
Colin Hendry	Dundee

For the Record

Record League victory:
9-0 v Middlesbrough, Division Two, November 6, 1954
Record Cup victory:
11-0 v Rossendale, FA Cup 1st Round, October 13, 1884
Record defeat:
0-8 v Arsenal, Division One, February 25, 1944
Record attendance:
61,783 v Bolton, FA Cup 6th Round, March 2, 1929
Most League points (2 for a win):
60, Division Three, 1974-75
Most League points (3 for a win):
89, FA Carling Premiership, 1994-95
Most League goals:
114, Division Two, 1954-55
Highest League scorer in season:
Ted Harper, 43, Division One, 1925-26
Most League goals in total aggregate:
Simon Garner, 168, 1978-92
Most Capped player:
Bob Crompton, 41, England
Most League appearances:
Derek Fazackerley, 596, 1970-86
Record Transfer Fee received: £1,400,000 from Manchester United for David May, June 1994
Record Transfer Fee paid: £5 million to Norwich for Chris Sutton, July 1994

ROVERS

Top Ten Strikers

Alan Shearer	1992-
Chris Sutton	1994-
Simon Garner	1978-1992
Ted Harper	Pre-war
Kevin Gallacher	1993-
Mike Newell	1991-
Eddie Quigley	1951-55
Howard Gayle	1987-91
Noel Brotherston	1977-86
Fred Pickering	1959-63, 1970-71

Top Ten Managers

Kenny Dalglish	1991-
Don Mackay	1987-91
Howard Kendall	1979-81
Thomas Mitchell	1884-96*
R.B. Middleton	1903-25
Johnny Carey	1953-58, 1970-71
Eddie Quigley	1967-70
Bobby Saxton	1981-86
Jack Marshall	1960-67
Jim Smith	1975-78

*Secretary-Manager

BLACKBURN ROVERS

Top League Scorers 1994-95

Alan Shearer	34
Chris Sutton	15
Mark Atkins	6
Tim Sherwood	6
Jason Wilcox	5
Colin Hendry	4
Graeme Le Saux	3
Paul Warhurst	2

Premiership Record 1994-95

Date	Opponent		Result
Aug 20	SOUTHAMPTON	(a)	D1-1
Aug 23	LEICESTER	(h)	W3-0
Aug 27	COVENTRY	(h)	W4-0
Aug 31	ARSENAL	(a)	D0-0
Sep 10	EVERTON	(h)	W3-0
Sep 18	CHELSEA	(a)	W2-1
Sep 24	ASTON VILLA	(h)	W3-1
Oct 01	NORWICH	(a)	L1-2
Oct 09	NEWCASTLE	(a)	D1-1
Oct 15	LIVERPOOL	(h)	W3-2
Oct 23	MAN UTD	(h)	L2-4
Oct 29	NOTTM FOR	(a)	W2-0
Nov 02	SHEFF WED	(a)	W1-0
Nov 05	TOTTENHAM	(h)	W2-0
Nov 19	IPSWICH	(a)	W3-1
Nov 26	QPR	(h)	W4-0
Dec 03	WIMBLEDON	(a)	W3-0
Dec 10	SOUTHAMPTON	(h)	W3-2
Dec 17	LEICESTER	(a)	D0-0
Dec 26	MAN CITY	(a)	W3-1
Dec 31	C.PALACE	(a)	W1-0
Jan 2	WEST HAM	(h)	W4-2
Jan 14	NOTTM FOR	(h)	W3-0
Jan 22	MAN UTD	(a)	L0-1
Jan 28	IPSWICH	(h)	W4-1
Feb 01	LEEDS	(h)	D1-1
Feb 05	TOTTENHAM	(a)	L1-3
Feb 12	SHEFF WED	(h)	W3-1
Feb 22	WIMBLEDON	(h)	W2-1
Feb 25	NORWICH	(h)	D0-0
Mar 04	ASTON VILLA	(a)	W1-0
Mar 08	ARSENAL	(h)	W3-1
Mar 11	COVENTRY	(a)	D1-1
Mar 18	CHELSEA	(h)	W2-1
Apr 01	EVERTON	(a)	W2-1
Apr 04	QPR	(a)	W1-0
Apr 15	LEEDS	(a)	D1-1
Apr 17	MAN CITY	(h)	L2-3
Apr 20	C.PALACE	(h)	W2-1
Apr 30	WEST HAM	(a)	L0-2
May 08	NEWCASTLE	(h)	W1-0
May 14	LIVERPOOL	(a)	L1-2

Roll of Honour

Premiership Champions
1994-95;
Division One Champions
1911-12, 1913-14;
Division Two Champions
1938-39;
Division Three Champions
1974-75;
FA Cup Winners
1884, 1885, 1886, 1890, 1891, 1928;
Full Members' Cup Winners
1986-87

Alan Kelly

THE FA CUP: Magic or Misery?

THE history of the FA Cup Final is full of romantic stories, of great goals, heroic deeds and unfortunate errors. No matter how a player performs on the big day at Wembley, at least he has the satisfaction of having played there on English soccer's biggest day of the season. But spare a thought for the unlucky ones who did not make it...

Sorry son, you're out!

Imagine scoring in every round of the competition - seven of your club's 15 goals on the way to the Twin Towers - and then being dropped for the Final.

It happened to Welsh international Ken Leek in 1960 when Leicester left him out against Spurs, and lost 2-0.

Leek was not the only unlucky Leicester player. In 1949, when City got to Wembley for the first time, they had to take on Wolves without star forward Don Revie, later the Leeds and England manager, and goalkeeper Ian McGraw, who had played in all the previous rounds.

Revie had injured his nose and lost so much blood on the day before the match that he was too ill to go to the game, let alone play.

McGraw had to watch while nursing a broken finger. Not surprisingly, Wolves proved too strong, winning 3-1.

Anfield agony

Bob Paisley, who was to win more trophies as a manager than any other in English history, knew the heartbreak of missing a Wembley Final.

He played in all rounds for Liverpool in 1950, and even scored fin the Semi against Everton, but was left out of the Wembley side who lost 2-0 to Arsenal.

Another Liverpool player, Gordon Milne, missed the club's first Cup Final victory in 1965, because of injury - 27 years after his father, Jimmy Milne, had dropped out of the Preston side for the same reason. By one of the many coincidences Cup Final history produces, the Liverpool manager in '65 was Bill Shankly. In '38 he had been a team-mate of Milne senior, and was godfather to Gordon.

Don Revie

The Matthews Final

ROY HARTLE missed the celebrated "Matthews Final" of 1953 after one of soccer's quickest rises to the Wembley threshold.

He made his debut for Bolton on January 1 that year and played in all their Cup matches until the Final, when Johnny Ball was preferred against Blackpool.

Bolton, 3-1 up, could not hold on with nine fit men and lost 4-3 to a Blackpool team which included Cyril Robinson, a late replacement for the injured Hugh Kelly.

Robinson picked up a winner's medal from his very first FA Cup-tie, while Kelly missed out after being a loser in two previous Finals.

Scottish international Allan Brown missed the match, too, with a broken leg. Poor Brown - injury had kept him out of the Blackpool team in 1951, as well.

When he eventually reached the Final, with Luton in 1959, he finished on the wrong end of a 2-1 result.

Liverpool's Gordon Milne (right) missed
the 1965 Cup Final through injury

Crooks was robbed

IN MORE recent times, Paul Reaney (Leeds), Alan Hudson (Chelsea), Bob Wilson (Arsenal), and Remi Moses (Manchester United) have all been kept out by injury, and three captains, Glenn Roeder (QPR), Wilf Rostron (Watford) and Steve Foster (Brighton) all missed a Final through suspension.

But perhaps the least fortunate would-be Wembley hero of all was Sammy Crooks, who spent more than 20 years with Derby and won 26 England caps at a time when there were far less international matches than these days. In 1946, the 38-year-old Crooks helped his club to get to Wembley for the first and only time, but an injury sustained in scoring the winning goal in the Sixth Round prevented him from playing in the winning team at Wembley. How unlucky can you get?

Dave Watson

Glenn Roeder

Steve Foster

THICK?
DON'T YOU BELIEVE IT

A COMMON criticism of footballers is that "they've got their brains in their boots." True, sometimes, but not always. There are a few exceptions...as we discovered...

Tony Galvin, twice an FA Cup winner with Spurs in the 1980s, had an honours degree in Russian which he took while studying at Hull University before going into soccer full-time.

His one-time playing colleague at White Hart Lane, Ossie Ardiles, qualified in law from a university at Cordoba in his native Argentina.

Phil Neale of Lincoln, who also played county cricket for Worcestershire, studied Russian while at Leeds University.

Liverpool's Steve Heighway and Brian Hall were known as "Big Bamber" and "Little Bamber" during their playing days, after TV quizmaster Bamber Gascoigne.

Heighway had graduated from Warwick with a degree in economics, and Hall had taken science at Liverpool.

Three Ipswich players of recent vintage - Steve Palmer, Phil Whelan and Clive Baker - also went to that seat of learning, and so did Maurice Cox of Torquay.

Ceri Evans, a New Zealander who played for Oxford United, was a university student. Not surprisingly, he went to Oxford.

Manchester United and England winger Steve Coppell, later a prominent manager, graduated in economics from Liverpool, and United and Newcastle striker Alan Gowling graduated in the same subject from Manchester.

Gordon Taylor, now head of the Professional Footballers Association, studied economics at Manchester, and former Fulham defender, John Lacy, took the same subject at London.

Paul Power of Manchester City studied law at the local university, took his degree, and almost gained an FA Cup winner's medal in 1981, when he captained his club in the Final.

Unfortunately for him, that other eagle, Ossie Ardiles, was on the opposing side...

Three former stars with plenty up top and degrees to prove it...Steve Heighway (left), Alan Gowling (below) and Steve Coppell (above).

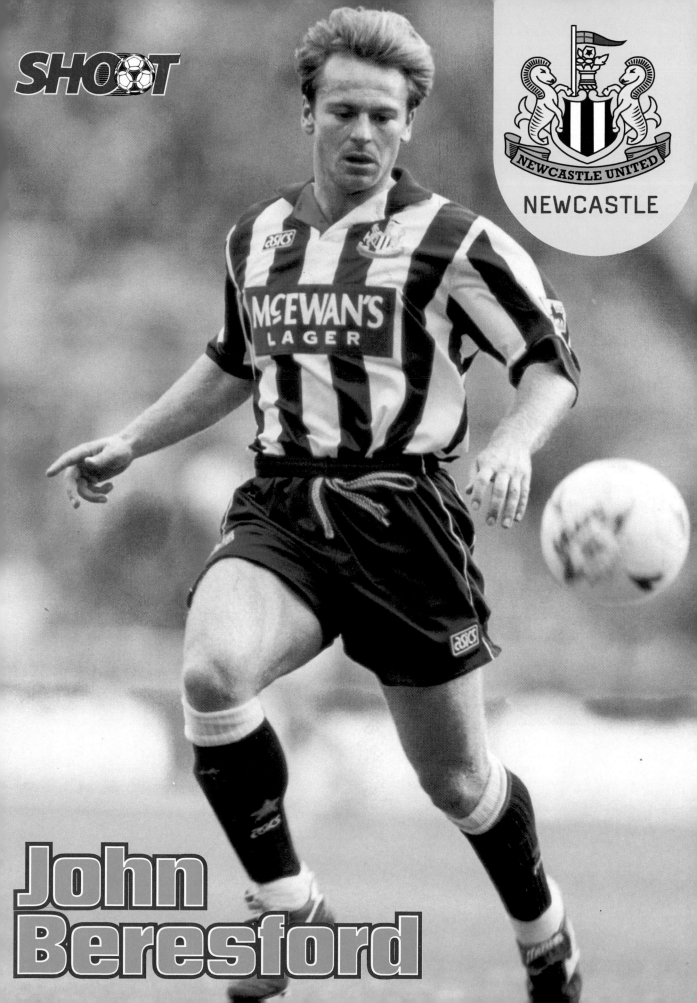

CELEBRITY

We put six soccer

COLIN CALDERWOOD
Tottenham

DARYL SUTCH
Norwich

LEE CLARK
Newcastle

FAVOURITE/WORST GROUND: No worst one but Old Trafford is my favourite – really special.

FAVOURITE/WORST GROUND: I don't like small grounds. My favourite is Carrow Road because of the fans, but I love Old Trafford, a great place.

FAVOURITE/WORST GROUND: My favourite has to be St. James' Park without doubt. The worst? Oxford – I never seem to get the right result there.

FAVOURITE PLAYER: I didn't have a special hero when I was young, but I think Jurgen Klinsmann has to be one of my favourites now.

FAVOURITE PLAYER: Definitely John Barnes. I used to watch him as much possible to learn.

FAVOURITE PLAYER: Lots – Chris Waddle, Peter Beardsley, Kevin Keegan, Gazza – all Newcastle players.

BIGGEST DISAPPOINTMENT: Haven't had one really, except perhaps to see Swindon relegated.

BIGGEST DISAPPOINTMENT: Our form this year took a dive but hopefully that is my worst disappointment.

BIGGEST DISAPPOINTMENT: Not being able to play when I am injured. It drives me crazy!

TOUGHEST OPPONENT: Balakov of Sporting Lisbon and Bulgaria. I couldn't get near him.

TOUGHEST OPPONENT: Stuart Pearce of Forest. Hardly anything gets past him.

TOUGHEST OPPONENT: None are easy. Alan Shearer is very difficult.

AMBITION: To play for Scotland in the 1996 European Championship finals.

AMBITION: To win as many honours as possible with Norwich City.

AMBITION: To win the FA Cup and Premiership with Newcastle, and to be in the England team.

TEAM SUPPORTED: I have always followed Stranraer, my local side. I still do.

TEAM SUPPORTED: It used to be Ipswich when I was younger! But I am a Norwich man now all the way.

TEAM SUPPORTED: There's always been only one for me – Newcastle! Who else?

SQUARES
stars in the hot seat

NIALL QUINN	JASON WILCOX	PAUL FURLONG
Republic of Ireland	**Blackburn**	**Chelsea**

FAVOURITE/WORST GROUND: My favourite has to be Maine Road, with Lansdowne Road a close second. Worst is Old Trafford for obvious reasons.

FAVOURITE/WORST GROUND: Ewood Park and Wembley are my favourites. The worst was Millwall's old Den. It was a very difficult place to play.

FAVOURITE/WORST GROUND: I don't mind where I play but my favourite ground is Wembley. I played there for Enfield in the FA Trophy Final.

FAVOURITE PLAYER: Johnny Giles was always my hero. I used to pretend to be him when I was still at school.

FAVOURITE PLAYER: John Barnes and Chris Waddle are my heroes, with Waddle having the edge. I also like Lothar Matthaus and Roberto Baggio.

FAVOURITE PLAYER: My idol is Glenn Hoddle. I never dreamed that one day I would play alongside him.

BIGGEST DISAPPOINTMENT: Missing out on a Championship medal – so far!

BIGGEST DISAPPOINTMENT: When we played in the Wembley Play-Off Final. I had to miss the game because of injury. That was a real choker.

BIGGEST DISAPPOINTMENT: Missing goals I should score. Going out of the European Cup-Winners' Cup Semi-Final by one goal was a real blow.

TOUGHEST OPPONENT: Tony Adams – a really good mate but very difficult to play against.

TOUGHEST OPPONENT: All of them! Players like Stuart Pearce. Fair but very hard.

TOUGHEST OPPONENT: When I was with Watford I remember playing against Gerry Taggart of Barnsley. He has to be the toughest.

AMBITION: To win a League Championship and get the medal that I missed out on when I was with Arsenal.

AMBITION: To win everything with Blackburn but the ultimate must be to win the World Cup with England, that would be great.

AMBITION: My dream is to play for England at the highest level.

TEAM SUPPORTED: Leeds – but only because Johnny Giles played for them!

TEAM SUPPORTED: I've always followed Blackburn although I come from Bolton and have a soft spot for them – except if we play them!

TEAM SUPPORTED: I was brought up a Spurs fan. I come from that area and love playing against them.

THE LIFE AND TIMES OF ANDY COLE

NOTTINGHAM

This is where it all began. Andy was born here on October 15th, 1971. Like most of his pals he grew up to love football and became a fan of both Nottingham Forest and Arsenal, who had won the double in the year he was born.

Andy played for his school and was then selected for his district. He trained with Forest before going to the FA School of Excellence. While there, he played for the England Under-15 side and hit four goals in nine games.

Arsenal were tipped off and when they took a look, they liked what they saw. In 1985 he signed schoolboy forms for them before becoming an apprentice in 1988.

ANDY COLE! ANDY COLE! ANDY, ANDY COLE!...when he gets the ball, he scores a goal, Andy, Andy Cole. You know you've made it big when the fans write a song about you. And they don't come any bigger than the £7m Man. Utd superstar...

LONDON

Andy liked London. He loved Highbury and enjoyed the life of the big city. He learned fast and stepped up onto the international scene to become a member of the England youth team. Steadily he progressed through the ranks to the fringe of the first-team.

On December 29th, 1990, George Graham decided to give Cole his senior debut. He came on as a sub with just five minutes to go in Arsenal's 4-1 win over Sheffield United. Ironically, it was the only five minutes of League action that Andy was to play for The Gunners.

On August 10th, 1991 it looked as if Andy was in for a good season. He was in Arsenal's side for the Makita tournament and again for the Charity Shield match against Spurs, a 0-0 draw. He waited for the call to League action when the season started but it did not come. Instead, he was loaned to Fulham where he scored four goals in 15 games, including his first-ever senior goal against Stoke on September 14th.

BRISTOL

After his loan spell at Fulham, Andy returned briefly to Highbury. But then came a loan request from Bristol City. Andy agreed to go and that decision completely changed his career. He made his loan debut for them on March 14th 1992, and in 12 loan games scored eight goals.

While still technically an Arsenal player, Andy was promoted to the England Under-21 side in May 1992 and scored in a 2-2 draw away to Hungary. By now, he was becoming a cult figure in Bristol and they wanted him to stay.

In July 1992, City boss Denis Smith persuaded his directors to break the club's transfer record by spending £500,000 on Andy . It was a great investment because Andy hit 17 goals in 32 games between August and March. Then his journey continued onwards and upwards.

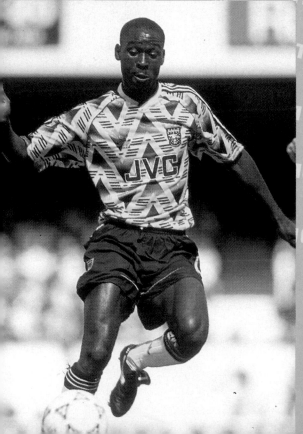

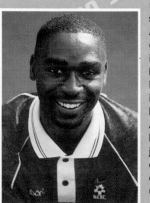

COLE

NEWCASTLE

Kevin Keegan knows a good player when he sees one and he didn't need to look twice at Andy Cole. He signed him on March 12th, 1993 for £1.75 million, which was a transfer record for both clubs. The following day Andy made his debut. Only a year earlier he had made his Bristol City debut on loan.

Andy was in the spotlight at Newcastle and he did not disappoint, hitting 12 goals in 12 games to play his part in Newcastle winning the 1992-93 First Division title. He liked Newcastle and Newcastle liked him.

August 21st, 1993 was a special day for Andy. He scored his first ever Premiership goal - against Manchester United. It was also the start of a free-scoring run which led to him creating a new club record 41 goals. It also put him on the way to winning the PFA Young Player of the Year Award and the SHOOT/adidas Golden Shoe for his scoring feats.

On December 13th Andy played for the England B team in a 2-0 win over Eire. Fans began to demand that he be given a chance in the England first team. But the 1994-95 season saw Andy struggle a little at first. Various injuries were blamed, including shin splints. He was rested and came back sharper than ever.

THE LIFE AND TIMES OF ANDY COLE

MANCHESTER

It came as a shock to the entire soccer world when a surprise announcement said that Andy Cole had become a Manchester United player for £7 million, part of the deal including Northern Ireland international Keith Gillespie joining The Magpies. The transfer took place on January 10th, 1995.

Andy's debut for United was a tough one. Rivals Blackburn were the visitors but it was Manchester United who took the honours with a 1-0 win. Andy did not score on that day but he more than made up for it on February 4th when he scored five as United hammered a record nine goals past Ipswich. It took his personal goals tally past 100.

England manager Terry Venables was under great pressure to include Cole in his side for the friendly visit by Uruguay. Andy made it as far as the bench and then, with 19 minutes left, Venables gave the crowd what they wanted. Cole made his senior England debut as substitute for Teddy Sheringham. The large crowd stood up to applaud as he ran on to the pitch.

JOURNEY'S END?

Andy Cole is happy in Manchester but his journey is by no means at an end. He is still in his early 20s and he has the soccer world at his feet and his passport will show off a lot more stamps before he is finished.

SHOOT

THE CELTIC FOOTBALL CLUB 1888

CELTIC

CR SMITH

Paul McStay

Identity Parade

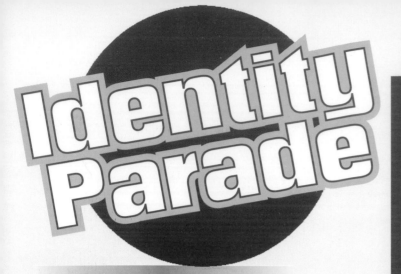

Re-arrange the letters for a top Premiership skipper.

CURVEE BEST

SHOOT QUIZ

STAR RIDDLE

How quickly can you identify this great star?

My surname was famous before I was born
My first name is Mark, I make keepers forlorn.
I now play for Rangers, I've been to Italy, too
I'm an ex-England star - and that's your last clue.

CAPITAL GOLD

Which Spurs star sounds as though he ought to be in the centre of things in Scotland?

GIVE US A CLUE

How many points can you score by guessing the name of this star as quickly as possible? Try it on your friends.

For five points - He was born in Newcastle.
For four points - He started his playing career with Carlisle.
For three points - He later played for Newcastle and Liverpool.
For two points - He has more than 50 England caps.
For one point - He now plays for Newcastle again

I'LL NAME THAT STAR...

Can you identify the soccer stars from the clues?

1. This great goalkeeper sounds like a sailor.
2. This Everton star sounds like a rabbit's home.
3. Former England star with a duck walk.
4. Manchester United star who sounds eager.
5. Blackburn star who is ice cool.

CAPITAL MOVES

We have "transferred" these six London Premiership club players. Can you you name them and place them in their correct strips?

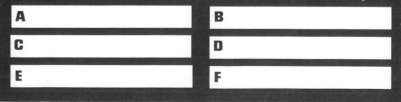

A	B
C	D
E	F

& PUZZLE SPECIAL

Can you name the star players in these various mini-puzzles?

WHAT DO YOU KNOW ABOUT...

ANSWERS PAGE 125

....MAN UNITED?

1. Who did Manchester United beat to win the European Cup in 1968?
A. Barcelona; B. Benfica or C. Bayern Munich
2. Who was manager before Alex Ferguson?
A. Dave Sexton; B. Ron Atkinson or C. Tommy Docherty
3. Who is United's top scorer of all-time?
A. George Best; B. Denis Law or C. Bobby Charlton
4. Since World War TWO, United have had one season out of the top division. Was it A.1974-75; B. 1979-80 or C. 1984-85?
5. United once won a European Cup tie 10-0. Who were they playing?
A. Lyn (Oslo); B. Anderlecht or C. Galatasary

....RANGERS?

1. Rangers signed Ally McCoist from which club?
A. Sunderland; B. St Mirren or C. St. Johnstone
2. Where was skipper Richard Gough born?
A. Sweden; B. South Africa or C. Scotland
3. Which European competition have Rangers won?
A. European Cup; B. European Cup-Winners' Cup or C. UEFA Cup
4. Who was manager before Graeme Souness?
A. Jock Wallace; B. John Greig or C. Alex Ferguson
5. Which team did Rangers beat in their last Scottish FA Cup win?
A. Dundee United; B. Celtic or C. Aberdeen

STAR TRAIL

Which England player started with Wolves, then went to Southampton and later joined Blackburn Rovers?

Richard Gough

TAKE A LETTER

Follow the clues to find the name of a Premiership goal ace.

Letter 1. This is the initial of the team which plays at Molineux.
Letter 2. The Coventry boss's first name begins with this.
Letter 3. You should have two of these in your face.
Letter 4. Half a horse?
Letter 5. Initial of Chelsea manager's surname.

Letter 6. When you've done this, go and have a cuppa.

What do you know about

Tony Yeboah?

Answer these posers on the popular Leeds United striker?

1. From which club did he join Leeds — Stuttgart, Eintracht Frankfut or Werder Bremen?
2. Name the country he represents in internationals — Zambia, Ghana or Morocco?
3. Against which club did he score a hat-trick last season — Ipswich, Leicester or Chelsea?

TYNESIDE TEASER

I am a Magpie and an animal, too.
You might even find me in your local zoo
I like to make runs into the penalty box
You'll know my name because it rhymes with socks!

MY GREATEST GAME

The stars reveal their most memorable matches

David White

Leeds

"Surprisingly it is not an international or a Cup Final, but a game between Oldham and Newcastle. It was early in the 1993-94 season at Boundary Park and it was a brilliant game. Newcastle won 3-1 and Peter Beardsley was fantastic with superb goal that put the icing on the cake."

Ian Crook

Norwich

"I can think of a lot of games I have enjoyed watching but one that I'll never forget is one I played in for Norwich. It was the UEFA Cup game away to Bayern Munich. We beat them 2-1, the first time they had ever lost at home to a British club. Fantastic!"

Ian Brightwell

Man. City

"My most memorable game was in 1989 when we beat Manchester United 5-1 (above). It was the first League derby game for a while because we had been out of the top division. It was a moment to savour and a great game."

Justin Edinburgh

Spurs

"My favourite has to be the 1991 FA Cup Final at Wembley (right). After Gazza was injured we were in a bit of a state of shock for a few minutes but then we realised we had nothing to lose so we just went for it. We ended up beating Forest 2-1 and getting the Cup from Princess Di."

Lee Clark

Newcastle

"I enjoyed playing in the game when we beat Leicester 7-1 after clinching promotion a couple of years ago, but the best game I have ever seen was when Liverpool beat Forest 5-0 at Anfield. The combination of John Barnes and Peter Beardsley in that match was just brilliant."

WHAT's the greatest game of football you have ever seen - or perhaps played in? Everyone has their favourites, even the stars themselves, that's why we asked them. And we got some great answers...

Steve Bruce
Man. United

"There have been some great games over the years. Often the ones you think are going to be great turn out not to be. Beating Chelsea 4-0 at Wembley to clinch the double - when I got the Cup (right) - will take some beating. That would be my favourite."

Steve Chettle
Forest

"My favourite game is one I played in. It was the 1990 Littlewoods Cup Final at Wembley. We beat Oldham 1-0 and it was a better game then the score might suggest. I think I had a good game so I have happy memories of that one."

Tony Adams
Arsenal

"If I had to pick just one game it would probably be the game at Anfield at the end of the 1988-89 season (above). We had to win by a couple of goals to take the title. Nobody thought that we would, but we did."

Ian Rush
Liverpool

The Cup games, the European games and some internationals stick in my mind. The Mersey ` derbies are always great and if I had to pick one it might be the 1986 FA Cup Final (left). We beat Everton 3-1, I scored two and by winning we did the double."

CLUES ACROSS

1. Not all my score is taken into account for a multi-million pound striker (anag) 4-9

8. His first managerial success was to take Swindon into the Premiership (6)

9. Country for whom Carlos Valderrama is their star (8)

10. The title of Mr Barrett at Everton (4)

11. Reading's American goalie could be Polish! (anag) (6)

12+14D. One of Ruud Gullit's previous clubs (3-9)

13. Where The Railwaymen are stationed (5-9)

17. Hull in red change at Barnet's ground (anag) (9)

18. He took over from Atkinson as boss at Aston Villa (6)

20. Former Liverpool and Scotland star, now a Match Of The Day pundit (6)

21. Hristo -, deadly Bulgarian striker who joined Barcelona from CSKA Sofia (9)

24. England star takes part in the main celebrations (4)

25. Andy - , joined Manchester City from Bury in 1991 (4)

26. First name of England's manager during 1966 World Cup triumph (3)

27. Find the connections for Montrose's ground at - Park (5)

28. - Heinz Rummenigge has twice been voted European Footballer Of The Year (4)

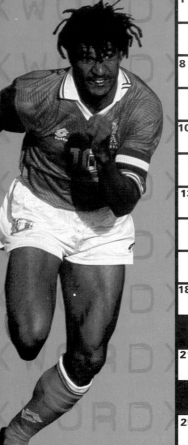

CLUES DOWN

1. International goalkeeper for Denmark (10)

2. Belgium's top club (10)

3. The kind of kick that most players look up to? (8)

4. Preston player gets right into a Lulu cassette (5)

5. Country that were in Wales' European Championship group (7)

6. (See 26 down)

7. Club based in Edinburgh (4)

12. Everton player gets his apron all mixed up with the sink (anag) (9)

14. (See 12 across)

15. Chelsea's Erland Johnsen plays for this country (6)

16. Grimsby Town play their home games at - Park (8)

19. They're arranged by clubs to assess promising youngsters (6)

22. Birmingham man gets stuck into pasta Italian style (4)

23. They're known as The Tigers (4)

24. Club based in Gothenburg (3)

26+6D. Liverpool beat them to win the 1984 European Cup Final (2-4)

Compiled by Trevor Hungerford

WORDSEARCH

```
G O L D E N M A R K S M A N
D S K A D E S I H T B O L E
E W I F A T L K U D G F S A
R E U G C O M A C A S R M D
A S P E C H E V I T A L Y W
L T U R L K O O W I L J E N
E G F I G T P L I F D N I G
D E M R S B A S L R C A V E
Y R O U A E L O M A P O H G
A M C T D N F H T S N U A C
V A Y N A H C C S I E D O K
I N O I N U T E I V O S N A
G Y E K A T V Z R Z B R I P
P D S B N E O C A H L A C S
```

Hidden in the above grid are the names of 8 previous winners of the European Championship. Names can go across to the left or right, up or down, or diagonally.

SOVIET UNOIN
SPAIN
ITALY
CZECHOSLOVAKIA
WEST GERMANY
FRANCE
HOLLAND
DENMARK

Roberto Baggio

JUVENTUS

RANGERS

For the Record

Record victory: 14-2 v Blairgowrie, Scottish Cup 1st Round, January 20, 1934
Record defeat: 2-10 v Airdrie, 1886
Record attendance: 118,567 v Celtic, Division One, January 2, 1939
Highest League scorer in season: Sam English, 44, Division One, 1931-32
Most League goals in total aggregate: Bob McPhail, 233, 1927-39
Most Capped player: George Young, 53, Scotland
Most League appearances: 496, John Greig, 1962-78

Record Transfer Fee received: £5,580,000 from Marseille for Trevor Steven, August 1991
Record Transfer Fee paid: £4.5m to Lazio for Paul Gascoigne, July 95

Rangers are, quite simply, the most successful Scottish club in history.

Records show that they have won more League Championships than any other side north of the border and they have also won more domestic trophies.

And, at the present time, their dominance is such that they are virtually untouchable.

Last season they claimed their seventh successive League title and they show no signs of taking their foot off the pedal.

Some people suggested that their best days were behind them when Graeme Souness quit the club to return to Liverpool but, if anything, Walter Smith has taken them to even greater heights.

He has won the title in every season he has been in charge, led Rangers to a domestic treble in 1992-93, and also to the final stages of the European Cup in the same year.

And the gap between Rangers and the rest is growing ever larger, with even Celtic struggling to stay in their slipstream.

Rangers' Glasgow rivals finished a massive 18 points behind Walter Smith's side last term, and even The Bhoys' Scottish Cup win was little consolation.

It is the League crown that really matters and that has become the exclusive property of Ibrox in the 1990s.

Continued ov

RANGERS

Top Ten Strikers

Ally McCoist	1983-
Mark Hateley	1990-
Davie Cooper	1977-89
Derek Johnstone	1970-83, 85-86
Willie Thornton	1936-1954
Jim Baxter	1960-65
Mo Johnston	1989-92
Kevin Drinkell	1988-90
Robert Fleck	1984-88
Andy Gray	1988-89

Top Managers

Graeme Souness	1986-91	
Walter Smith	1991-	
John Grieg	1978-83	
Jock Wallace	1972-78,	1983-86
William Wilton	1899-1920	
Bill Struth	1920-54	
Scot Symon	1954-67	
Davie Whyte	1967-69	
Willie Waddell	1969-72	

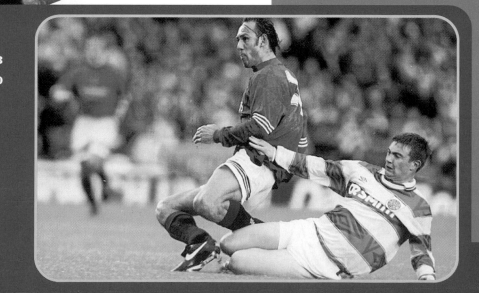

Top Ten Transfers

PLAYER	FROM
Ally McCoist	Sunderland
Mark Hateley	Monaco
Stuart McCall	Everton
Chris Woods	Norwich
Paul Gascoigne	Lazio
Terry Butcher	Ipswich
Andy Goram	Hibernian
Richard Gough	Tottenham
Jim Baxter	Raith
Davie Cooper	Clydebank

Roll of Honour

League Champions
45 times (from 1890-91 to 1994-95)

Scottish Cup Winners
26 times (from 1893 to 1993)
45 times (from 1890-91 to 1994-95)

League Cup Winners
19 times (from 1946-47 to 1993-94)

Premiership Record 1994-95

Date	Opponent		Result
Aug 13	MOTHERWELL	(h)	W2-1
Aug 20	PARTICK	(a)	W2-0
Aug 27	CELTIC	(h)	L0-2
Sep 11	HEARTS	(h)	W3-0
Sep 17	FALKIRK	(a)	W2-0
Sep 24	ABERDEEN	(a)	D2-2
Oct 01	DUNDEE UTD	(h)	W2-0
Oct 08	HIBS	(a)	L1-2
Oct 15	KILMARNOCK	(h)	W2-0
Oct 22	MOTHERWELL	(a)	L1-2
Oct 30	CELTIC	(a)	W3-1
Nov 05	PARTICK	(h)	W3-0
Nov 09	HEARTS	(a)	D1-1
Nov 19	FALKIRK	(h)	D1-1
Nov 25	ABERDEEN	(h)	W1-0
Dec 04	DUNDEE UTD	(a)	W3-0
Dec 10	KILMARNOCK	(a)	W2-1
Dec 26	HIBS	(h)	W2-0
Dec 31	MOTHERWELL	(a)	W3-1
Jan 04	CELTIC	(h)	D1-1
Jan 07	PARTICK	(a)	D1-1
Jan 14	FALKIRK	(a)	W3-2
Jan 21	HEARTS	(h)	W1-0
Feb 04	DUNDEE UTD	(h)	D1-1
Feb 12	ABERDEEN	(a)	L0-2
Feb 25	KILMARNOCK	(h)	W3-0
Mar 04	HIBS	(a)	D1-1
Mar 11	FALKIRK	(h)	D2-2
Mar 18	HEARTS	(a)	L1-2
Apr 01	DUNDEE UTD	(a)	W2-0
Apr 08	ABERDEEN	(h)	W3-2
Apr 16	HIBS	(h)	W3-1
Apr 20	KILMARNOCK	(a)	W1-0
Apr 29	MOTHERWELL	(h)	L0-2
May 07	CELTIC	(a)	L0-3
May 13	PARTICK	(h)	D1-1

Top League Scorers 1994-95

Player	Goals
Hateley	13
Laudrup	10
Durie	5
Durrant	4
Huistra	3
McCall	3
Miller	3
Robertson	3
Boli	2
Mikhailichenko	2
McLaren	2
Moore	2

SHEFF. WED

SHOOT

Des Walker

SHOOT

Goal Matt Jackson

Everton v Tottenham

High Flyers!

Meet soccer's international jet set

THEY are the high-flying football heroes - the guys who have travelled from afar to take centre stage in the world's greatest soccer competitions - the English and Scottish Premier Divisions. Let's meet some of the jet-set superstars.

GERMANY has been well represented in England during the last year. **JURGEN KLINSMANN** was the chief superstar, a shock signing by Spurs who lit up their season and won over the fans with his sheer exuberance for the game, coupled with brilliant skills and a flair for goals that would charm even the most cynical of supporters.

"I wanted to find out what English football was like and I did. The English League is the best in Europe. It was fantastic to play in stadiums with such a brilliant atmosphere. I enjoyed every minute of it and I was deeply honoured to receive the Footballer of the Year award," said Jurgen.

His countrymen, **UWE ROSLER** and **MAURIZIO GAUDINO**, have been performing wonders for Manchester City. And let's not forget **UWE FUCHS** who helped Middlesbrough win the First Division Championship and with it a place in the Premiership.

HOLLAND has also had a great ambassador in English soccer during the last year in **BRIAN ROY**, who linked up with Nottingham Forest after the 1994 World Cup for £2.8m, making him one of the most expensive of the Premiership imports.

"I came to the City Ground for talks and fell in love with the club. I just had to join and sample English football. It has been great," said Roy, who is by no means the only Dutchman playing in this country. Another World Cup star new to England was **JOHN DE WOLF** and there are at least another nine Dutch players.

In Scotland, the giant **PIERRE VAN HOOYDONK** also flew in to make his mark for Celtic, while at the other end of Glasgow a Frenchman and a Dane hit the headlines as **BASILE BOLI** and **BRIAN LAUDRUP** performed for Rangers. Laudrup proved to be the hit of the year north of the border.

"My family and I took to Scotland straight away. It is

Brian Roy

a beautiful country and we love it. Playing for Rangers has also been a thrill because it is one of the biggest clubs in the world and I am sure we will soon make a big impression in Europe," said Laudrup. But he's not the only great Dane in Britain, perhaps the best known being Manchester United's Peter Schmeichel, whose record speaks for itself.

NORWAY has provided the most imports from Europe with a dozen or so players in English soccer. Names like **STIG BJORNEBYE**, who

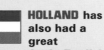
Jurgen Klinsmann

Roy Wegerle

Pierre Van Hooydonk

Uwe Rosler

broke his leg just after playing his part in Liverpool's Coca-Cola Cup triumph over Bolton at Wembley.

"I used to watch English football on Norwegian television all the time and I was a big Liverpool fan long before I ever had the chance of joining them. It was a dream come true and I still have to keep pinching myself," said Stig, whose countrymen include **HENNING BERG** of Blackburn, **ERIK THORSTVEDT** of Spurs, **ERLAND JOHNSEN** of Chelsea, **ALF-INGE HAALAND** of Nottingham Forest and others.

THE UNITED STATES have sent us a few stars as well - **JOHN HARKES** and **KASEY KELLER** of Derby and Millwall respectively may not be performing in

Erland Johnsen

the Premiership but their presence is still felt. A surprise signing was that of **COBI JONES** by Coventry. Jones, famous for his exploded pipe-cleaners hairstyle, settled in well to Premiership soccer, helped by fellow USA World Cup squaddie **ROY WEGERLE**.

BEST OF THE REST

Then, of course, there are the jet-setters from Africa. Nigeria has sent Everton's **DANIEL AMOKACHI**, while **TONY YEBOAH** of Leeds and Ghana proved himself to be a major coup for Howard Wilkinson, who said: "He's so strong and skilful I would place him among the top ten strikers currently in Europe. He's brilliant, a real nightmare for defenders." Zimbabwe's **PETER NDLOVU** is a real jet-setter, almost constantly flying backwards and forwards to play for Coventry and his country. At £10,000 he has to be the best import of them all.

But which country has the most representatives in English football? Believe it or not - Australia! There were 15 at the last count doing their stuff over here, **TONY DORIGO** of Leeds and Aston Villa goalkeeper **MARK BOSNICH** being the best known. Bosnich, who cost Villa absolutely nothing, loves England but is an Australian through and through - he even leaps about like a kangaroo and flies through the air like a boomerang. And he is always on form both Home and Away - just ask his Neighbours!

QUITE a number of footballers have shared their names with other people - some of them pretty famous...

NEVILLE CHAMBERLAIN, for example, was Prime Minister of Great Britain during the 1930s - and no relation to the England and Stoke City winger of the 70s.

Likewise Harold Wilson of Burnley and Preston was not related to the HAROLD WILSON (below) who was Prime Minister around the same time in the '60s.

American President JIMMY CARTER (left) had no connection with the Jimmy Carter of Millwall, Liverpool and Arsenal, and Bobby Kennedy had nothing to do with the Manchester City player who was around at the same time.

GORDON RICHARDS, one of the most celebrated jockeys in history, had a namesake who played outside-left for Wrexham and Chester in the 1960s.

PETER SCOTT was an artist who became head of the

FAMOUS N
But not who you think they are

World Wildlife Fund, and another Peter Scott played for various clubs and for Northern Ireland in the 1970s.

BERNARD SHAW, the Irish writer, had a soccer "rival" in the England Under-23 full-back of the same name, who played for both Sheffield clubs and for Wolves.

Similarly West Brom goal keeper JOHN OSBORNE (right) had a playwright double in John "Angry Young Man" Osborne (inset).

BADEN POWELL, founder of the Boy Scout movement, had a namesake who played for Darlington for a time during the 1950s.

American comedian DANNY THOMAS had a namesake player in Danny Thomas of Coventry and Spurs, who won two caps for England but was forced to retire in 1987, through injury, when still only 26.

Soul singer BARRY WHITE (left) is a famous showbiz name. But who remembers the Barry White who kept goal for Hull in the 70s?

And JIM BOWIE, inventor of the Bowie knife and defender of The Alamo, had a replica in the little Scottish forward of Chelsea, Fulham and Brentford.

Didn't know that, did you?

AMES

THE TOON

WHAT makes Geordie fans so special? Everyone who plays at Newcastle will tell you the same thing - that Geordie fans are just that - FANatics! Even when their team is suffering they still turn up in their thousands. Here's what the stars think of the Toon Army...

"The fans here are simply amazing. Kids are brought up expecting to see 34,000 at a game. We don't get those sort of crowds and atmosphere at internationals in Czechoslovakia. To play in front of the St. James's Park crowd is more special to me as a player than perhaps those people in that crowd."
PAVEL SRNICEK

"It is incredible up here. Even when I go down the road to get a paper the fans get their autograph books out. It's a fanatical do-or-die sort of thing for them. There are not many clubs that can say 7,000-odd fans travel to all their away games. They are by far the best supporters I have ever played in front of."
DARREN PEACOCK

"The supporters here are a different breed. It's hard to describe the passion they have for the game, it's religion to them. They take defeat even harder than the players. At some away matches where the home crowds are fairly small, the Toon Army transforms the place into a sea of black and white - it's a tremendous sight."
BARRY VENISON

"Almost everyone you meet up here is football mad. When you go out you are instantly recognised and people always want to come up and talk to you about football. They're great and you have to talk to as many of them as you can."
ROBERT LEE

"The fans here are like nowhere else. They get behind you even before you arrive at the ground. It can be like having a couple of extra players in the side. They will you on and can pick you up and carry you when you are worn out. They are the best."
KEVIN KEEGAN

Oh no, they're not...

OF COURSE, other players think the world of their own fans and while they will admit that the Geordie supporters are special, they still believe their own fans are the best...

"I was not prepared for the sort of fanaticism on Merseyside. I knew the people in Liverpool were something else but I didn't know how much. I got a great reception when I started here and in the street I even had Liverpool fans wishing me all the best. The fans here are just unbelievable."
VINNY SAMWAYS (Everton)

"Our fans are some of the loudest and most loyal in Britain and I'm sure opposing teams will find it more and more fearful to come to Stamford Bridge as the ground development is completed and the crowds get larger and louder."
JOHN SPENCER (Chelsea)

ARMY'S TOPS

"The Rangers support is just incredible. The crowds are huge and they follow you all over the place. It is like a gigantic family. Everyone is related by the fact that they follow Rangers. They are fanatics and will stay with you all the way, kicking every ball."
MARK HATELEY (Rangers)

"I always thought the Feyenoord fans were the best in Europe until I came to Molineux. I got a great welcome from the fans. Clearly Wolves are no ordinary team, they are a major club with tremendous support. I never realised that before I came to England."
JOHN DE WOLF (Wolverhampton)

"Manchester United fans are something very different. They have been marvellous to me and made me feel at home. I love to play at Old Trafford and I love the fans. They are very loud, very exciting and very loyal. I love them."
ERIC CANTONA (Man. United)

"The Liverpudlians are great people who take their football seriously, although the Scouse sense of humour comes through. The rivalry is intense but I've never come up against any hostility from Evertonians. Liverpool fans are legendary throughout the world and they live up to it."
PHIL BABB (Liverpool)

NOTTM
FOREST

Stan Collymore

SUPER STADIUMS

THE European Championship comes to England in 1996 and, as well as a quarter of a million foreign fans flooding into the country, there will be many more watching on TV. The spotlight will be well and truly on the English soccer scene and the grounds being used for this great occasion.

The super stadiums to be used have been carefully chosen by the Football Association and all will be at their shining best when the tournament starts on June 8th, 1996. Let's check out the arenas where the gladiators will vie for the honour of emerging the best in Europe...

ANFIELD

Home of Liverpool Football Club and certainly not a strange name to the top guns of European soccer. Anfield narrowly got the vote over neighbouring Goodison Park. Liverpool have been at Anfield since they were formed in 1892, ironically after Everton fell out with their landlord, who owned Anfield. Everton went to Goodison and Liverpool were formed to fill the gap. Anfield has been the scene of much domestic and European drama over the years and the 41,000 capacity crowds that flock to the European games at this completely revamped stadium will no doubt be as thrilled to be at one of the most famous stadiums in the world as the players. The Kop may have gone, but the spirit lives on.

VILLA PARK

Aston Villa are eagerly looking forward to their share of Euro '96. Villa have been at the ground since 1897 and it has seen high drama during its long and great history. Today the capacity is 46,000 and that includes the largest behind-the-goal seating area in Europe, with about 15,000 fans able to sit where they once stood. In March 1946 a record 76,588 crowd watched Villa play Derby in the FA Cup. There won't be crowds of that size at Villa Park ever again but the noise from the fans will certainly sound like it.

CITY GROUND

Nottingham Forest's new look City Ground has one of the most beautiful settings in the country and will certainly look good on the TV shots with its views of the River Trent. It was in 1898 that the City Ground became home to Forest. There were some great European nights during the Clough regime and manager Frank Clark has led his men back into Europe in a very short space of time. The icing on the cake will be the Euro '96 games next summer. The capacity for the City Ground these days is 31,000, all seated in the lap of luxury.

HILLSBOROUGH

Sheffield Wednesday have for many years owned one of the top grounds in the country, regularly chosen for major matches, including the 1966 World Cup finals. International soccer returns in the summer to a ground that has been revamped and now seats just over 36,000. For the record, the 1966 World Cup group held at Hillsborough included West Germany, Argentina, Spain and Switzerland. The Germans won the group and went on to win their Quarter-Final against Uruguay on the same pitch. The Germans clearly won't mind if they play their Euro games at Hillsborough.

ELLAND ROAD

Fans watching on television will have a perfect view of the world's largest cantilever stand. The TV cameras are situated directly opposite this awesome stand in what has developed into one of the finest grounds in Europe. Leeds United have been at Elland Road since they came into existence in 1920, and it is hard to imagine that the club was borne out of Leeds City, which went bankrupt. Today, Elland Road is an arena of modern technology with all the trappings of a highly successful club. Gone are the dark old days of hooliganism at Elland Road – hopefully for good – and Euro '96 games are a fitting reward for the work the club has done.

ST. JAMES' PARK

Newcastle could have sold their tickets over and over again during the last few seasons. The stadium is regularly packed by the Geordie fans who are arguably the most fervent in the land. The club is on the up and crowds of 35,000-plus have regularly filled the ground. And they will be packing it again when the Euro show hits town. Since 1892, The Magpies have been at St. James' Park, but they have never sampled international soccer on this scale before and you can guarantee they will make the most of it.

OLD TRAFFORD

The Theatre of Dreams. That's how they describe Old Trafford these days. Ticket demands outweigh availability week after week and it is planned to push the stadium capacity up to 54,500 by building extra tiers on what is already a magnificent stadium. Manchester United's ground is famous throughout the world and is a mecca for fans visiting England, even if they have no interest in European football. Apart from a spell at Maine Road when their ground was war damaged, United have been at Old Trafford since 1910. Millions upon millions of pounds have been spent on the ground – and it shows.

WEMBLEY

Wembley is, of course, the palace of big occasions. Countless major matches of all sports have been held in the world famous stadium for decades. It has become an institution in the history of the game. There will be more history made on Sunday 30th June when the Final of the 1996 European Championship takes place. A capacity crowd will flock to see if England can repeat the success of 30 years previously. On that occasion, the capacity crowd saw England win the World Cup for the first time and some of those present then will be there again next summer to see if England can win the European title for the first time. It promises to be an absolute feats of football and all European eyes will be on the hallowed turf next June as Wembley proves itself once again to be a superstar among superstadia.

The wonder of WEMBLEY

10 fab facts about the venue of legends

1. Most football fans know that the first FA Cup Final to take place at Wembley was in 1923 when Bolton beat West Ham - but what about when was the first Football League Cup Final held at Wembley? It was 1967 when QPR beat Middlesbrough 3-2.

2. Wembley opened in 1923 and remained a 100,000-capacity until the late 1980s when both end terraces were seated. It now holds 80,000 seats.

3. England have been playing internationals at Wembley since 1924, when they drew 1-1 with Scotland. But they didn't play regularly there until the 1960s, preferring to travel the country and play London matches at Highbury.

4. Very few players have scored a hat-trick at Wembley. Geoff Hurst's trio in the World Cup Final in 1966 is the most famous but Everton striker Paul Rideout scored three there for England schoolboys against Scotland in 1980.

5. The FA Amateur Cup Final often attracted 100,000 fans to Wembley but its' replacement, the FA Trophy, usually sees around 20,000 fans watch England's top non-League sides in action.

6. The 1995 Auto Windscreens Shield Final saw more fans pack into Wembley than the Coca-Cola Cup Final between Liverpool and Bolton a few weeks earlier. A staggering 76,663 saw Birmingham beat Carlisle in extra time - over a thousand more than the 'bigger' game.

7. Stockport County must hate the sight of Wembley - they reached the Twin Towers four times between 1991-94 and lost every time! Twice in the Play-Offs and twice in the Autoglass Trophy Final.

8. Manchester United, Liverpool and Arsenal are all very familiar with the Twin Towers - they all share the record of playing in 17 Cup Finals at Wembley, not to mention numerous Charity Shield matches. Everton have reached 12 Wembley Finals in various competitions, Spurs ten.

9. Wembley staged American Football matches for ten years. The annual American Bowl, featuring NFL teams, was replaced by the World League in 1991, when the London Monarchs went all the way to the World Championship in front of big Wembley crowds.

10. Wembley, of course, was the stage for England's only World Cup triumph to date - a 4-2 victory against West Germany back in 1966. But will England be 'running round Wembley with the Cup' when the great stadium hosts the 1996 European Championship Final?

CONQUERORS OF EUROPE

THANKS to France, we are in for a feast of football in 1996. Why France? Because that is where the idea of a European Championship first started. Just as it was a Frenchman who came up with the idea for the World Cup; so it was a Frenchman - Henry Delaunay, secretary of the French FA - who invented the European equivalent. Already we are counting the days until it all begins - on Saturday 8th June, 1996. It is the greatest soccer occasion this country will have seen for 30 years and yet it had fairly humble beginnings when no British teams took part.

1960 Hosts: France Winners: Russia

FRANCE were justifiable hosts in 1960 when the competition made its debut. Politics were soon involved as Spain withdrew because of Russian involvement in their civil war more than 25 years earlier!

Russia (right) had the last laugh though. They reached the Final and, on July 10th 1960, they became the very first winners of he European Championship when they beat Yugoslavia 2-1 in Paris in front of 17,996 fans.

1964 Hosts: Spain Winners: Spain

FOUR years soon passed and it was Euro finals time again - this time with Spain as hosts.

England entered for the first time with Alf Ramsey taking over as boss midway through the qualifiers. England failed, but the host country did not.

In front of 120,000 fans in Madrid's Chamartin Stadium they won 2-1. Their victims? Russia! The 1964 finals established the competition as one to take seriously.

1968 Hosts: Italy Winners: Italy

ITALY were the next hosts of the competition in 1968. The Home Championship was used as a qualifying group which England won, although they did not reach the Euro Final. That honour was left to hosts Italy (above) who drew 1-1 with Yugoslavia in Rome but then beat them 2-1 in the replay two days later. Some 135,000 fans watched the two games.

SHOOT looks back at the

1972 Hosts: Belgium
Winners: W. Germany

THE show moved on to Belgium for 1972. Mighty West Germany were now on the glory trail and made it all the way to the Final, where they met Russia who were in their third Final - not bad out of four attempts. The Germans proved too strong for the Russians and the fans celebrated through the night in Brussels after their 3-0 win.

1976 Hosts: Yugoslavia
Winners: Czechoslovakia

THE 1976 finals were held in Yugoslavia. It took a penalty shoot-out to decide the winner after Czechoslovaia and West Germany thrilled 30,790 fans in a 2-2 draw in Belgrade. It was the Germans who shed tears at the end of it after the mighty Czechs won 5-3 on penalties, following extra-time.

1980 Hosts: Italy
Winners: West Germany

EUROPEAN soccer went back to Italy in 1980. Once again the British clubs failed to make much impression and it was left to West Germany (right) to take the honours for a second time. Their first success was in Belgium. This time it was against Belgium, beating them 2-1 in a close Final in Rome in front of 47,860 fans.

1984 Hosts: France
Winners: France

FRANCE hosted the 1984 finals and stole the show in front of their own fans. They played some great football and stormed to the Final where they faced the threat of past winners Spain.

But it was the Frenchmen who swept all before them and thrilled the 47,368 fans in Paris with a masterly 2-0 victory - inspired by Michel Platini (right) - to take for the first time the competition they had invented.

history of the Euro Championship

CONQUERORS OF EUROPE

1988 Hosts: Germany
Winners: Holland

HOLLAND had been threatening to win a tournament for some years but tended to miss out at the death. But that was not the case in 1988 when the finals were held in West Germany.

Surprisingly, the hosts did not make it to the Final - but Holland did.

Their opponents were the Soviet Union. It became the Gullit (right)

and Van Basten show as the two Dutchmen scored a goal each to take the trophy, applauded by an appreciative 62,770 crowd in Munich.

1992 Hosts: Sweden
Winners: Denmark

THEN came 1992. Not for the first time, England flopped in the finals. Scotland and the Republic of Ireland emerged with honours, but not THE honour. That was left to Denmark (below) who beat Germany 2-0 in the Final in Sweden's Ullevi Stadium. But the Danes should not have been there, only being included as substitutes for politically-troubled Yugoslavia.

1996 Hosts: England
Winners:?????

AND so to 1996. Can England get their name on the trophy at last? Will mighty Germany or Italy walk away with the honours again? Will there be a surprise as there was four years ago? Only time will tell. But one thing is guaranteed - there will be thousands of winners watching the games.

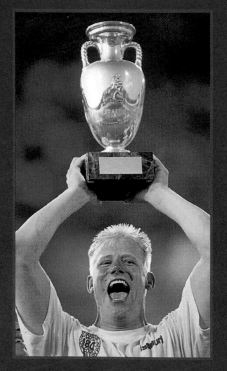

DID YOU KNOW?

•The very first European qualifying game took place on September 28th, 1958. Henri Delaunay, who dreamed up the competition, died shortly before.

•In February 1968, Scotland played England at Hampden Park in a Euro qualifier. A crowd of 134,461 attended. It was a 1-1 draw.

•Spain needed to beat Malta by 11 goals to qualify for the 1984 finals. They won 12-1!

•In the 1984 finals, Michel Platini of France hit a competition record of nine goals.

•Host countries have won the Championship three times out of nine.

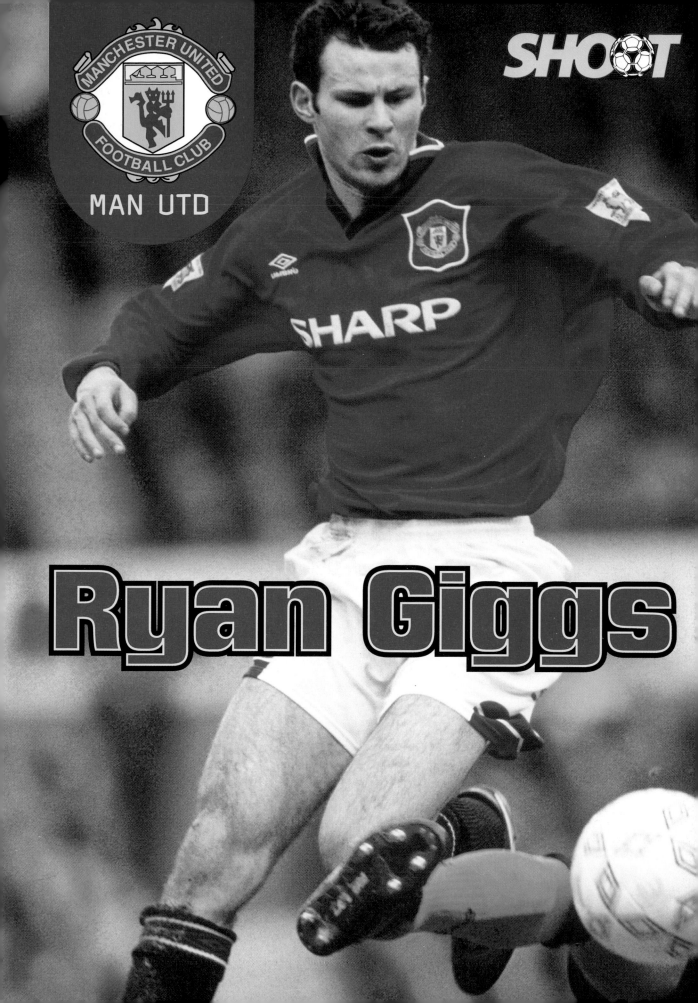

MANCHESTER UNITED FOOTBALL CLUB

MAN UTD

SHOOT

Ryan Giggs

MANCHESTER

Manchester United are, arguably, the most famous club in the world.

From Matt Busby's Babes to the golden era of Charlton, Best and Law, up until the present time and Alex Ferguson's all-conquering heroes, the very name Manchester United has been synonymous with all that is good in football.

They have always played the game with skill and panache - and have picked up dozens of trophies along the way.

Alex Ferguson is already the club's most successful manager, other than the great Sir Matt, and it seems that he, and his side, are destined to rule for a while yet.

Fergie has had his share of critics over the years and in 1990 was on the verge of the sack at Old Trafford. But the board of directors stood by him and how they have been rewarded.

They were crowned as the first Premier League Champions in 1992-93 - their first title triumph for 26 years - and followed that a year later by becoming only the fourth team this century to do the 'double'.

And even last term, when they finished the season empty handed, they were only two games, and probably two goals, from claiming a unique 'double double'.

Top Ten Transfers

PLAYER	FROM
Andy Cole	Newcastle
Peter Schmeichel	Brondby
Paddy Crerand	Celtic
Brian McClair	Celtic
Arnold Muhren	Ipswich
Ray Wilkins	Chelsea
Bryan Robson	West Brom
Roy Keane	Nottm Forest
Lee Sharpe	Torquay
Denis Law	Torino

For the Record

Record League victory:
10-1 v Wolves, Div 1, Oct 15, 1892;
9-0 v Ipswich, Prem, Mar 4, 1995
Record Cup victory:
10-0 v RSC Anderlecht, European Cup Preliminary Round, second-leg, September 26, 1956
Record defeat:
0-7 v Blackburn, Division One, April 10, 1926
Record attendance:
76,962, Wolves v Grimsby, FA Cup Semi-Final, March 25, 1939
Most League points (2 for a win):
64, Division One, 1956-57
Most League points (3 for a win):
92, FA Premier League, 1993-94
Most League goals:
103, Division One, 1956-57 and 1958-59
Highest League scorer in season:
Dennis Viollet, 32, 1959-60
Most League goals in total aggregate:
Bobby Charlton, 199, 1956-73
Most Capped player:
Bobby Charlton, 106, England
Most League appearances:
Bobby Charlton, 606, 1956-73
Record (domestic) Transfer Fee received:
£2 million from Coventry for Dion Dublin, September 1994
Record Transfer Fee paid:
£7,000,000 to Newcastle for Andy Cole, January 1995

UNITED

Top Ten Strikers

Bobby Charlton	1956-72
Denis Law	1962-72
George Best	1963-73
Andy Cole	1995-
Tommy Taylor	1952-57
Eric Cantona	1992-
Mark Hughes	1983-85, 1988-
Ryan Giggs	1990-
Frank Stapleton	1981-86
Lou Macari	1972-83

Top Ten Managers

Sir Matt Busby	1945-69
Alex Ferguson	1986-
Ron Atkinson	1981-86
Dave Sexton	1977-81
Tommy Docherty	1972-77
Ernest Magnall	1900-12
Scott Duncan	1932-37
Jimmy Porter	1938-44
Herbert Bamlett	1927-31
John Robson	1914-21

MANCHESTER UNITED

Roll of Honour

Premier League Champions
1992-93, 1993-94;
Division One Champions
1907-08, 1910-11, 1951-52, 1955-56,
1956-57, 1964-65, 1966-67;
Division Two Champions
1935-36, 1974-75;
FA Cup Winners
1909, 1948, 1963, 1977, 1983, 1985,
1990, 1994;
League Cup Winners
1992;
European Cup Winners
1968;
European Cup-Winners' Cup
Winners 1992

Premiership Record 1994-95

Aug 20	QPR	(h)	W2-0
Aug 22	NOTTM FOREST	(a)	D1-1
Aug 27	TOTTENHAM	(a)	W1-0
Aug 31	WIMBLEDON	(h)	W3-0
Sep 11	LEEDS	(a)	L1-2
Sep 17	LIVERPOOL	(h)	W2-0
Sep 24	IPSWICH	(a)	L2-3
Oct 01	EVERTON	(h)	W2-0
Oct 08	SHEFF WED	(a)	L0-1
Oct 15	WEST HAM	(h)	W1-0
Oct 23	BLACKBURN	(a)	W4-2
Oct 29	NEWCASTLE	(h)	W2-0
Nov 06	ASTON VILLA	(a)	W2-1
Nov 10	MAN CITY	(h)	W5-0
Nov 19	C.PALACE	(h)	W3-0
Nov 26	ARSENAL	(a)	D0-0
Dec 03	NORWICH	(h)	W1-0
Dec 10	QPR	(a)	W3-2
Dec 17	NOTTM FOR	(h)	L1-2
Dec 26	CHELSEA	(a)	W3-2
Dec 28	LEICESTER	(h)	D1-1
Dec 31	SOUTHAMPTON	(a)	D2-2
Jan 03	COVENTRY	(h)	W2-0
Jan 15	NEWCASTLE	(a)	D1-1
Jan 22	BLACKBURN	(h)	W1-0
Jan 25	C.PALACE	(a)	D1-1
Feb 04	ASTON VILLA	(h)	W1-0
Feb 11	MAN CITY	(a)	W3-0
Feb 22	NORWICH	(a)	W2-0
Feb 25	EVERTON	(a)	L0-1
Mar 04	IPSWICH	(h)	W9-0
Mar 07	WIMBLEDON	(a)	W1-0
Mar 15	TOTTENHAM	(h)	D0-0
Mar 19	LIVERPOOL	(a)	L0-2
Mar 22	ARSENAL	(h)	W3-0
Apr 02	LEEDS	(h)	D0-0
Apr 15	LEICESTER	(a)	W4-0
Apr 17	CHELSEA	(h)	D0-0
May 01	COVENTRY	(a)	W3-2
May 07	SHEFF WED	(h)	W1-0
May 10	SOUTHAMPTON	(h)	W2-1
May 14	WEST HAM	(a)	D1-1

Top League Scorers 1994-95

Andy Cole	21*
Andrei Kenchelskis	14
Eric Cantona	13
Mark Hughes	8
Paul Ince	5
Brian McClair	5
Paul Scholes	5
Lee Sharpe	3

(*9 with Newcastle)

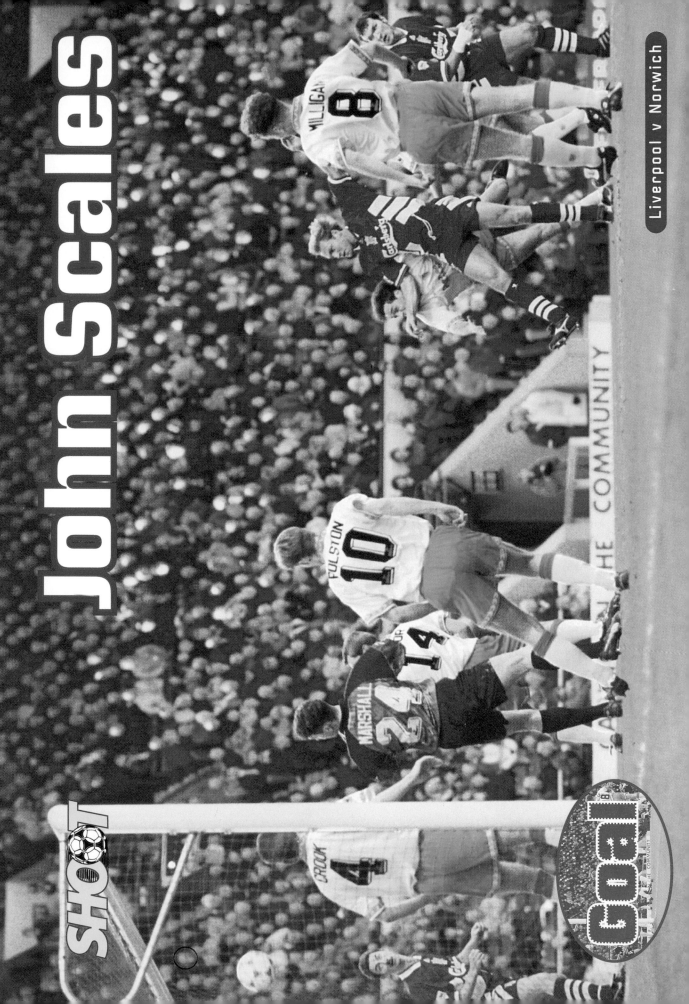

John Scales

SHOOT

Liverpool v Norwich

Goal

Tribute to the SHOOT boot boys
The GOLDEN GUYS

SHOOT/adidas Golden Shoe Awards 1994-95
ALAN SHEARER
Blackburn & England
TOMMY COYNE
Motherwell & Scotland

NOT MANY people have been given the boot and been absolutely delighted with it but the sort of boot we are talking about is something rather special. It means that you have hit the back of the net more times than anyone else during the season. We are talking about the SHOOT/adidas Golden Shoe, one of the most coveted prizes in the game. Let's look at some of the stars who have these magnificent trophies in their homes.

Back in 1982, the very first winner was Kevin Keegan who hammered home 26 goals in the old First Division - not for Newcastle or Liverpool, but for Southampton.

The Saints fans were delighted and so were the Celtic supporters north of the border because their main man, George McCluskey, took the award in Scotland, hitting 21 goals as his club strode to the Scottish Championship.

The names listed since that first award read like a who's who of soccer heroes. Two Scots and an Englishman have won the award three times. Ally McCoist and Tommy Coyne have stolen the honours in Scotland, while Gary Lineker still leads the pack of predators in England.

This season Alan Shearer's name has been added to the scroll of honour. The Blackburn and England star finished well ahead of his nearest rivals and adds the SHOOT/adidas Golden Shoe to his countless other prizes.

Over the border Tommy Coyne has completed his hat-trick. In 1988 he was with Dundee, in 1991 he was a Celtic player and in 1995 he took the award while banging in the goals for Motherwell, emulating Gary

Blackburn's Alan Shearer — present holder of the SHOOT/adidas Golden Shoe Award.

Shearer heads home against Sheffield Wednesday. He finally notched up 34 goals, equalling Andy Cole's Premiership record.

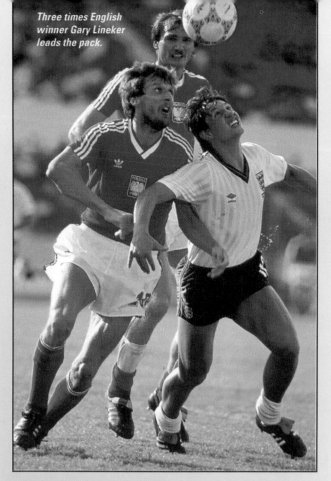

Three times English winner Gary Lineker leads the pack.

Kevin Keegan was first to win the award in 1981-82, when he was at Southampton.

ENGLAND:

	League goals
1981-82 Kevin Keegan (Southampton)	26
1982-83 Luther Blissett (Watford)	27
1983-84 Ian Rush (Liverpool)	32
1984-85 Kerry Dixon (Chelsea)	
Gary Lineker (Leicester)	24
1985-86 Gary Lineker (Everton)	30
1986-87 Clive Allen (Tottenham)	33
1987-88 John Aldridge (Liverpool)	26
1988-89 Alan Smith (Arsenal)	23
1989-90 Gary Lineker (Tottenham)	24
1990-91 Alan Smith (Arsenal)	23
1991-92 Ian Wright (Arsenal)	29
1992-93 Teddy Sheringham (Tottenham)	22
1993-94 Andy Cole (Newcastle)	34
1994-95 Alan Shearer (Blackburn)	34

SCOTLAND:

1981-82 George McCluskey (Celtic)	21
1982-83 Charlie Nicholas (Celtic)	29
1983-84 Brian McClair (Celtic)	23
1984-85 Frank McDougall (Aberdeen)	22
1985-86 Ally McCoist (Rangers)	24
1986-87 Brian McClair (Celtic)	35
1987-88 Tommy Coyne (Dundee)	33
1988-89 Mark McGhee (Celtic)	
Charlie Nicholas (Aberdeen)	16
1989-90 John Robertson (Hearts)	17
1990-91 Tommy Coyne (Celtic)	18
1991-92 Ally McCoist (Rangers)	34
1992-93 Ally McCoist (Rangers)	34
1993-94 Mark Hateley (Rangers)	22
1994-95 Tommy Coyne (Motherwell)	17

Lineker's feat of winning the honour with three different clubs.

In England, the club honours are shared between North London rivals Arsenal and Tottenham. They have both supplied the Golden Shoe winner on three occasions. In Scotland, Celtic are well ahead with six winners, four more than rivals Rangers.

Here is your complete check-list of winners from the top divisions north and south of the border...

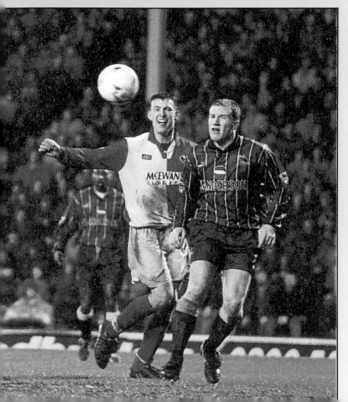

Rangers' Ally McCoist won his last award in 1992-93.

High flyer Tom Cruise in Top Gun.

Dirty Rotten Scoundrels st...

Action-man Arnold Schwarzenegger

Forest's Colin Cooper is a great fan of Tom Cruise in Top Gun.

SCREEN TEST
What's on TV in the homes of the stars?

NICK BARMBY of Tottenham likes gangster films and that's why he had no problem telling us his favourite films.

"I have three favourites - The Godfather, The Godfather II and The Godfather III. Three great films, well acted and tremendous stories. I can watch them over and over."

England skipper **DAVID PLATT** has never been much of a television fan and especially since moving to Italy he has found it even harder to get into TV. But, he enjoys a good film.

"I keep a library of films so that I have always got something to relax with. There are a number of English programmes on Italian television but they are nearly all dubbed and therefore it is difficult to relax with them because you are constantly working hard to understand what is being said. So I keep a film library and especially enjoy comedies. One of my favourites is Dirty Rotten Scoundrels - I just can't stop laughing at it."

Saints star Jason Dodd collects Arnold Schwarzenegger videos.

Nottingham Forest's **COLIN COOPER** is a romantic at heart and his favourite film has a connection with his wife, Julie. The film? Top Gun!

"I was heavily into Top Gun just before I met Julie and it has stayed with me ever since. I must have watched it 50 or 60 times and I enjoy it all over again everytime I see it."

JEREMY GOSS of Norwich City is a big fan of Robert De Niro, but it makes you wonder why. Does

WHEN they are not starring on TV themselves, who do the stars watch to help them unwind? SHOOT has all the answers...

he go to the cinema regularly?

"I haven't been for years," he says. Well then, is it videos? "I am not much of a video person. It was ages before I got around to getting one. I like De Niro from the films I have seen on television. There was a series of his films on Channel 4 and I became a fan."

Blackburn and England star **GRAEME LE SAUX** will watch most types of films but he is not so sure

Liverpool defender Neil Ruddock thinks David Jason is the business.

Jermemy Goss of Norwich likes Robert Di Niro movies on TV.

Michael Caine and Steve Martin.

Al Pacino as the mob boss, with Andy Garcia in the Godfather films.

Harrison Ford as Indiana Jones in The Last Crusade.

Comedies such as Dirty Rotten Scoundrels are David Platt's choice.

City's Tony Coton is an adventure film buff and watches Indiana Jones.

about television, although there is one series he particularly enjoys.

"I love Red Dwarf," he says. "I suppose it is escapism really. Whatever, I enjoy it. It has a great mixture of sci-fi and laughs."

Perhaps the greatest screen buff of them all is **TONY COTON.** The Manchester City goalie

often spends his spare time in multi-cinemas just switching screens between films and grabbing a quick bite of something as he goes.

"I like adventure stories mostly - Indiana Jones, Robin Hood, Dances With Wolves and that sort of thing. I enjoy relaxing and escaping with a good film. I am also keen on television and I follow the soaps, especially Coronation Street which I think is still a great programme."

What do you think Liverpool's **NEIL RUDDOCK** enjoys watching?

"When it is on television there is nothing to touch Only Fools and Horses. David Jason is brilliant as Del Boy. But I have another favourite that takes over as my No. 1 when Only Fools is off the screen - Crimewatch!"

Southampton's **JASON DODD** likes his movies to be action packed as you can see from his choice of favourites.

"I like a lot of Arnold Schwarzenegger films. Terminator was great, for instance. There's always plenty going on. I go to the movies a lot and I have heaps of videos at home so it is difficult to pick just one favourite. Any Arnie film or Bruce Lee film, plenty of action in them, too."

Dons' Stewart McKimmie likes cartoons and Four Weddings and a Funeral.

Award winning movie Four Weddings and a Funeral.

STEWART McKIMMIE of Aberdeen is into a different kind of entertainment.

"I'm really into Disney", he reveals. "The kids are a great excuse to go to see the movies or to buy the videos. We've got quite a collection now and I'm still adding to it. I've watched Aladdin loads of times. I like other films too - like Four Weddings And A Funeral - but I'm a big Disney fan. Those cartoons are great."

Blackburn's Graeme Le Saux likes most films, but loves sci-fi tales.

Spurs Nick Barmby rates The Godfather films as top entertainment.

Mark Hateley

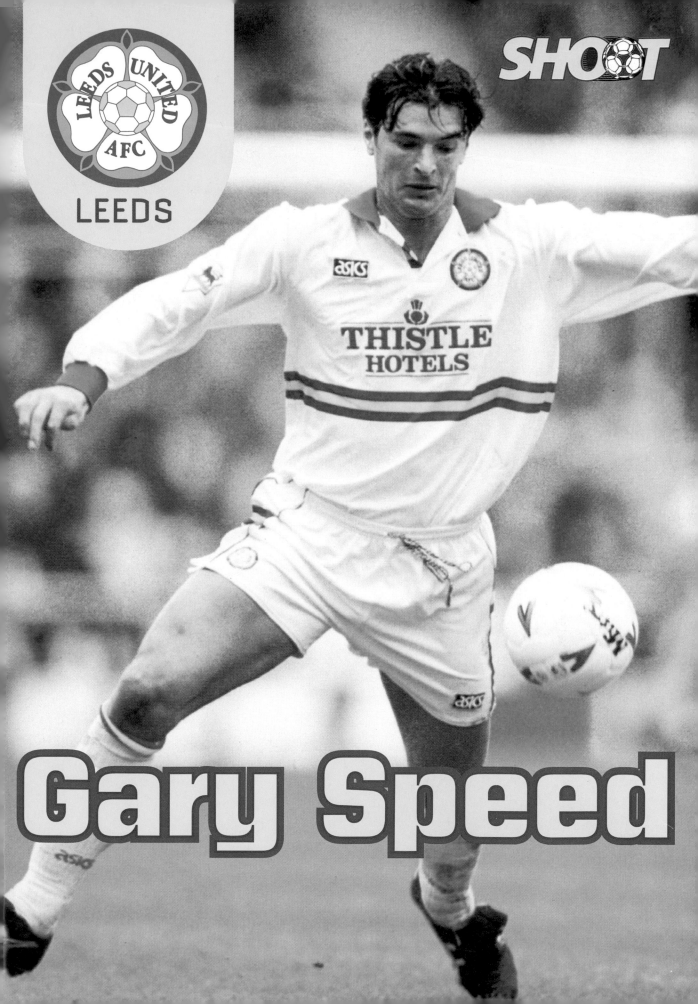

LEEDS UNITED AFC

LEEDS

SHOOT

THISTLE HOTELS

Gary Speed

MIDDLESBRO'

Jan Aage Fjortoft

CLUB FOCUS

No.4 Newcastle

NEWCASTLE

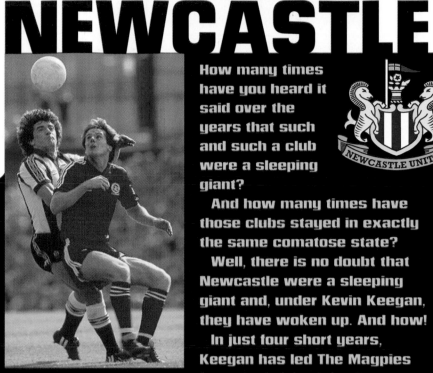

For the Record

Record League victory: 13-0 v Newport, Division Two, October 5, 1946

Record Cup victory: 9-0 v Southport, FA Cup 4th Round, February 1, 1932

Record defeat: 0-9 v Burton Wanderers, Division Two, April 15, 1895

Record attendance: 68,386 v Chelsea, Division One, September 3, 1930

Most League points (2 for a win): 57, Division Two, 1964-65

Most League points (3 for a win): 96, Division One, 1992-93

Most League goals: 98, Division One, 1951-52

Highest League scorer in season: Hughie Gallacher, 36, Division One, 1926-27

Most League goals in total aggregate: Jackie Milburn, 178, 1946-57

Most Capped player: Alf McMichael, 40, Northern Ireland

Most League appearances: Jim Lawrence, 432, 1904-22

Record Transfer Fee received: £7,000,000 from Manchester United for Andy Cole, January 1995

Record Transfer Fee paid: £6,000,000 to QPR for Les Ferdinand, June 1995

How many times have you heard it said over the years that such and such a club were a sleeping giant?

And how many times have those clubs stayed in exactly the same comatose state?

Well, there is no doubt that Newcastle were a sleeping giant and, under Kevin Keegan, they have woken up. And how!

In just four short years, Keegan has led The Magpies from the brink of the Second Division - a drop from which they would surely have never recovered - to the peak of the Premiership.

And now they are once again one of the major players in the English game and destined never to suffer such a dramatic fall from grace again.

It is almost certain that Keegan is the only man who could have turned the club around in such spectacular fashion. He is more than just a manager on Tyneside - he is a God!

As Peter Beardsley says: "He is simply the best. If it hadn't been for Kevin, I would never have come back to Newcastle."

The only thing missing for all Keegan's great work - and that of his right-hand man Terry McDermott - is a trophy in the St James' Park boardroom.

It surely won't be long in arriving.

Continued over...

NEWCASTLE

Top Ten Strikers

Andy Cole	1993-1995
Peter Beardsley	1983-86, 1993-
Kevin Keegan	1982-83
Malcolm Macdonald	1971-75
Hughie Gallacher	1925-1930
Jackie Milburn	1946-56
George Robledo	1948-52
Wyn Davies	1966-70
John Tudor	1970-76
Bryan 'Pop' Robson	1964-70

Top Ten Transfers

PLAYER	FROM
Andy Cole	Bristol City
Peter Beardsley	Everton
Malcolm Macdonald	Luton
Philippe Albert	Anderlecht
Warren Barton	Wimbledon
Kevin Keegan	Southampton
Chris Waddle	Tow Law Town
Barry Venison	Liverpool
George Robledo	Barnsley
Les Ferdinand	QPR

Premiership Record 1994-95

Date	Opponent		Result
Aug 21	LEICESTER	(a)	W3-1
Aug 24	COVENTRY	(h)	W4-0
Aug 27	SOUTHAMPTON	(h)	W5-1
Aug 31	WEST HAM	(a)	W3-1
Sep 10	CHELSEA	(h)	W4-2
Sep 18	ARSENAL	(a)	W3-2
Sep 24	LIVERPOOL	(h)	D1-1
Oct 01	ASTON VILLA	(a)	W2-0
Oct 09	BLACKBURN	(h)	D1-1
Oct 15	C.PALACE	(a)	W1-0
Oct 22	SHEFF WED	(h)	W2-1
Oct 29	MAN UTD	(a)	L0-2
Nov 05	QPR	(h)	W2-1
Nov 07	NOTTM FOR	(a)	D0-0
Nov 19	WIMBLEDON	(a)	L2-3
Nov 26	IPSWICH	(h)	D1-1
Dec 03	TOTTENHAM	(a)	L2-4
Dec 10	LEICESTER	(h)	W3-1
Dec 17	COVENTRY	(a)	D0-0
Dec 26	LEEDS	(a)	D0-0
Dec 31	NORWICH	(a)	L1-2
Jan 02	MAN CITY	(h)	D0-0
Jan 15	MAN UTD	(h)	D1-1
Jan 21	SHEFF WED	(a)	D0-0
Jan 25	WIMBLEDON	(h)	W2-1
Feb 01	EVERTON	(h)	W2-0
Feb 04	QPR	(a)	L0-3
Feb 11	NOTTM FOR	(h)	W2-1
Feb 25	ASTON VILLA	(h)	W3-1
Feb 28	IPSWICH	(a)	W2-0
Mar 04	LIVERPOOL	(a)	L0-2
Mar 08	WEST HAM	(h)	W2-0
Mar 19	ARSENAL	(h)	W1-0
Mar 22	SOUTHAMPTON	(a)	L1-3
Apr 01	CHELSEA	(a)	D1-1
Apr 08	NORWICH	(h)	W3-0
Apr 14	EVERTON	(a)	L0-2
Apr 17	LEEDS	(h)	L1-2
Apr 29	MAN CITY	(a)	D0-0
May 03	TOTTENHAM	(h)	D3-3
May 08	BLACKBURN	(a)	L0-1
May 14	C.PALACE	(h)	W3-2

Roll of Honour

League Champions
1904-05, 1906-07,
1908-09, 1926-27;
First Division Champions
1004-05, 1906-07, 1908-
09, 1926-27, 1992,93
FA Cup Winners
1910, 1924, 1932, 1951,
1952, 1955
Second Division
Champions
1964-65
Fairs Cup Winners 1968-69

Top Ten Managers

Arthur Cox	1980-84
Jim Smith	1988-91
Jack Charlton	1984-85
Frank Watt	1895-1932
Joe Harvey	1962-75
Bill McGarry	1977-80
Willie McFaul	1985-88
Ossie Ardiles	1991-92
Charlie Mitten	1958-61
Kevin Keegan	1992-

Top League Scorers 1994-95

Peter Beardsley	11
Ruel Fox	10
Paul Kitson	8
Andy Cole	7
Robert Lee	7
Steve Watson	3
Steve Howey	2
Philippe Albert	2
Keith Gillespie	2

David Platt continues to make a mockery of Manchester United's decision to release him as a youngster. Here's how he's done it...

DAVID'S CAREER

He was born in Chadderton on June 10th 1966, just six weeks before England's greatest moment - the day that skipper Bobby Moore received the World Cup.

Platt started life as a keen Manchester United fan and it was his dream to play for them one day - as well as for his country, of course.

And when his career began it seemed that his dream was going to come true - Manchester United signed him as an apprentice after he had impressed in schools matches.

Ron Atkinson, then manager at Old Trafford, later shattered Platt's hopes when he axed him during a staff-cutting exercise. David was ready to give up hope of a career in the game.

But Dario Gradi, a coach with a big reputation for getting the best out of young players, persuaded David to try again with Crewe. That was in February 1985 and it proved to be a turning point as Platt made his senior debut and went on to hit 61 goals in 152 games.

Other clubs started to take notice and Graham Taylor decided to take a gamble by signing Platt for Aston Villa for £200,000, in February 1988.

Bobby Robson was England manager then and after playing David in three Under-21 matches, gave him his first senior cap at Wembley on November 15th, 1989 in a 0-0 draw against Italy.

One of David's greatest moments was scoring the goal that put England into the Quarter-Finals of the 1990 World Cup.

David's international displays drew attention from Italy and, in July 1991, he was sold by Villa to Bari for £5.5 million.

He settled well in Italy and after a season he was snapped up by Juventus for £6.5 million.

Another year passed and he was on the move again, this time a £5.2 million deal taking him to Sampdoria where he has been ever since.

There has been much speculation about Platt returning to England but he is happy in Italy and looks like staying there for at least another two seasons.

On the international scene he was made England captain by Graham Taylor and that continued when Terry Venables took over as boss.

His goals have put him among the top six England scorers of all-time - and he hasn't finished yet!

Now Platt's

PLATT THE MAN:

David now speaks fluent Italian.

He enjoys pasta - both cooking and eating it - but he misses fish and chips and always has some when he returns to England.

He likes to play golf and cricket.

David is always in great demand for Italian TV shows.

He has a great sense of humour and often leads the England joke sessions.

At home in Italy he has a large collection of CDs and also a library of movies.

David is married and owns a piece of land near Macclesfield where he plans to live when he returns from Italy.

He still dreams about playing for Manchester United one day.

One of his treasured possession is the PFA Player of the Year Award which he won in 1990.

David has various business interests in England, including a restaurant.

When he retires from the game he would like to get involved in the media.

WORDS OF WISDOM:

"When he first came into the England team you could see he was going to be special - and he is. He has achieved a great deal and is still there doing it." PETER SHILTON

DAVID SAYS:

"It all seems a long way from the days at Crewe where I was very happy. I have never regretted any of the ups and downs or anything I have done in my career. I've still got a lot to do and I feel that I am good for several years yet. I could still be playing football in Italy in the year 2000.

"Of course, I want to come back to England eventually but I stress the word 'eventually'. I enjoy my trips to England and will look forward to coming home for good one day. But I am happy in Italy and my experience there helps a lot in playing for England. I hope to still be part of the set-up by the time the 1998 World Cup comes around."

Magic!

SHOOT plots the rise and rise of the England skipper

HOW IT STARTED:

It was back in 1891 when transfers started getting serious. The first three-figure deal went into the record books when Aston Villa paid West Bromwich Albion £100 for Willie Groves.

Ten years went past before the next milestone as Sunderland paid a record £500 to Sheffield United for Alf Common. In three years his value doubled, Middlesbrough paying £1,000 for him in February 1905.

In 1912, big spending Blackburn paid £2,000 for Danny Shea from West Ham and ten years after that The Hammers swelled their bank balance again when they sold Syd Puddefoot to Falkirk for a mind-blowing £5,000.

BIG MONEY:

There was a sharp intake of breath when transfers hit the five-figure mark for the first time as Arsenal paid £10,000 for **David Jack** (left) from Bolton in 1928, but it was more than 30 years before that figure began to seem insignificant.

Denis Law (below right) was on the scene and, in 1960, Manchester City paid Huddersfield £50,000 for him. But he was not finished there. In 1962 Law became Britain's first six figure star when Torino paid £100,000 for him.

Transfers hit the half-million pounds mark in 1979 when West Brom bought David Mills from Middlesbrough, but that record didn't last long as **Trevor Francis** (above right) joined Forest from Birmignham for £1m in February '79.

The transfer crown seems to have passed from Blackburn to Manchester United and back quite often in the last few years. As well as paying £2 million - a record for a goalkeeper - for **Tim Flowers** (right) from Southampton in November 1993, Kenny Dalglish

had spent a record £3.3 million for Alan Shearer from the same club in July 1992. That record was broken when Roy Keane joined United in July 1993 for £3.75m.

Blackburn reclaimed the record by paying Norwich £5 million for **Chris Sutton** (right) in July 1994. Then came Fergie's swoop for **Andy Cole** (below) in January 1995 - a cool £7 million.

RECORD

ANDY COLE became the most expensive star in British football when he joined Man United for £7m. Even Chris Sutton, Duncan Ferguson and several other mega-million superheroes paled by comparism. But where did it all begin? What would Andy Cole have cost a century ago? Here are a few clues....

SHOOT follows

BREAKERS

SKY'S THE LIMIT?

Not at the moment. The Football League suggested to the FA back in 1899 that there should be a transfer fee limit of £10. The League thought about it and NINE years later introduced a limit of £350. This restriction lasted just four months before it was abandoned. Since then transfer fees have run riot and will probably go on doing so.

ODD TRANSFERS:

* When Portsmouth signed Guy Whittingham (above) in 1989 they paid £450! That was to buy him out of the Army.
* In 1897, Sam Hollis became the first manager of Bristol City. He was given £30 to buy players. He demanded another £10 and was given it. With that he went out and bought EIGHT players!
* When Manchester United signed Hughie McLenahan from Stockport in 1927 the fee was three freezers of ice cream!
* When Torquay signed Ian Johnston from Whitley Bay a few years ago the fee was six footballs!

BRITAIN'S MOST EXPENSIVE:

David Platt is the costliest player Britain has produced - so far! He has been transferred from Crewe to Aston Villa to Bari to Juventus to Sampdoria. His total fees come to £17.4 million - and he has probably not finished yet!

WHAT THEY WOULD HAVE COST?

If they were playing 100 years ago these are the corresponding fees that today's stars would have cost their clubs:-

ANDY COLE - £1,000
CHRIS SUTTON - £750
DUNCAN FERGUSON - £600
ALAN SHEARER - £500

the transfer trail

ARSENAL

SHOOT

Ian Wright

LIVERPOOL

For the Record

Record League victory:
10-1 v Rotherham Town, Division Two, February 18, 1896
Record Cup victory:
11-0 v Stromsgodset Drammen, European Cup-Winners' Cup, 1st Round, 1st-leg, September 17, 1974
Record defeat:
1-9 v Birmingham, Division Two, December 11, 1954
Record attendance:
61,905 v Wolves, FA Cup 4th Round, February 2, 1952
Most League points (2 for a win): 68, Division One, 1978-79
Most League points (3 for a win): 90, Division One, 1987-88
Most League goals: 106, Division Two, 1961-62

Highest League scorer in season: Roger Hunt, 41, Division Two, 1961-62
Most League goals in total aggregate:
Roger Hunt, 245, 1959-69
Most capped player:
Ian Rush, 60, Wales
Most League appearances:
Ian Callaghan, 640, 1960-78
Record Transfer Fee received: £2,750,000 from Juventus for Ian Rush, June 1986
Record Transfer Fee paid:
£3,600,000 to Wimbledon for John Scales, August 1994; £3,600,000 to Coventry for Phil Babb, August 1994

Liverpool are poised to take the English game by storm again.

After a turbulent few years, the club which so dominated in the late 70s and early 80s looks set for a return to the glory days.

During those heady days under Bob Paisley, The Reds were virtually untouchable and the League Championship trophy was almost a permanent fixture at Anfield.

Joe Fagan and Kenny Dalglish followed suit before Graeme Souness's ill-fated reign at the club he served so well as a player.

Although he won the FA Cup in 1992, his time at the helm will not be remembered fondly, either by himself or the fans.

But now, under the guiding hand of Roy Evans, The Kop can again look forward to the future with optimism.

Evans is a graduate from the famed Anfield Boot Room and has knowledge in abundance. And although it will surely be asking too much for The Reds to dominate as they did during those golden Paisley years, there is at last something to look forward to again.

Evans led them to glory last season in the Coca-Cola Cup, there is no doubt that they will be up there challenging Manchester United and Blackburn for the major honours.

Continued over...

LIVERPOOL

Top Ten Transfers

PLAYER	FROM
Ian Rush	Chester
Kevin Keegan	Scunthorpe
Ray Clemence	Scunthorpe
Graeme Souness	Middlesbrough
Emlyn Hughes	Blackpool
John Toshack	Cardiff
Ron Yeats	Dundee United
Kenny Dalglish	Celtic
Phil Neal	Northampton
John Barnes	Watford

Top Ten Managers

Billy Shankly	1959-74
Bob Paisley	1974-83
Joe Fagan	1983-85
Kenny Dalglish	1985-91
Graeme Souness	1991-94
Roy Evans	1994-
Tom Watson	1896-1915
George Patterson	1928-36
George Kay	1936-51
Don Welsh	1951-56

Top Ten Strikers

John Toshack	1970-77
Billy Liddel	1946-60
Kevin Keegan	1971-76
Ian Rush	1980-86, 1988-
Robbie Fowler	1994-
Roger Hunt	1959-69
Kenny Dalglish	1977-89
Ian St John	1961-70
Peter Beardsley	1987-90
John Aldridge	1986-89

Roll of Honour

Division One Champions
1900-01, 1905-06, 1921-22, 1922-23,
1946-47, 1963-64, 1965-66, 1972-73,
1976-77, 1978-79, 1979-80, 1981-82,
1982-83, 1983-84, 1985-86, 1987-88,
1989-90;
Division Two Champions
1893-94, 1895-96, 1904-05, 1961-62;
FA Cup Winners
1965, 1974, 1986, 1989, 1992;
League Cup Winners
1981, 1982, 1983, 1984, 1995
European Cup Winners
1977, 1978, 1981, 1984.
UEFA Cup Winners
1973

Premiership Record 1994-95

Aug 20	C.PALACE	(a)	W6-1
Aug 28	ARSENAL	(h)	W3-0
Aug 31	SOUTHAMPTON	(a)	W2-0
Sep 10	WEST HAM	(h)	D0-0
Sep 17	MAN UTD	(a)	L0-2
Sep 24	NEWCASTLE	(a)	D1-1
Oct 01	SHEFF WED	(h)	W4-1
Oct 08	ASTON VILLA	(h)	W3-2
Oct 15	BLACKBURN	(a)	L2-3
Oct 22	WIMBLEDON	(h)	W3-0
Oct 29	IPSWICH	(a)	W3-1
Oct 31	QPR	(a)	L1-2
Nov 05	NOTTM FOR	(h)	W1-0
Nov 09	CHELSEA	(h)	W3-1
Nov 21	EVERTON	(a)	L0-2
Nov 26	TOTTENHAM	(h)	D1-1
Dec 03	COVENTRY	(a)	D1-1
Dec 11	C.PALACE	(h)	D0-0
Dec 18	CHELSEA	(a)	D0-0
Dec 26	LEICESTER	(a)	W2-1
Dec 28	MAN CITY	(h)	W2-0
Dec 31	LEEDS	(a)	W2-0
Jan 02	NORWICH	(h)	W4-0
Jan 14	IPSWICH	(h)	L0-1
Jan 24	EVERTON	(h)	D0-0
Feb 04	NOTTM FOR	(a)	D1-1
Feb 11	QPR	(h)	D1-1
Feb 25	SHEFF WED	(a)	W2-1
Mar 04	NEWCASTLE	(h)	W2-0
Mar 14	COVENTRY	(h)	L2-3
Mar 19	MAN UTD	(h)	W2-0
Mar 22	TOTTENHAM	(a)	D0-0
Apr 05	SOUTHAMPTON	(h)	W3-1
Apr 09	LEEDS	(h)	L0-1
Apr 12	ARSENAL	(a)	W1-0
Apr 14	MAN CITY	(a)	L1-2
Apr 17	LEICESTER	(h)	W2-0
Apr 29	NORWICH	(a)	W2-1
May 02	WIMBLEDON	(a)	D0-0
May 06	ASTON VILLA	(a)	L0-2
May 10	WEST HAM	(a)	L0-3
May 14	BLACKBURN	(h)	W2-1

Top League Scorers 1994-95

Robbie Fowler	25
Ian Rush	12
Steve McManaman	8
John Barnes	7
Jamie Redknapp	3
Jan Molby	2
Neil Ruddock	2
John Scales	2

Warren Barton, the pride of London...err, Newcastle!

Below: What are you doing Tony? You'll do yourself a mischief if you're not careful! Above: Shoe shine, sir?

"You've

This town ain't big enough for the both of us. Auf Wiedersehen, Jurgen!

Been Framed"

And than I spent three seasons with the French Foreign Legion...

This little lot should make you feel at home at The Bridge, Ruud!

RUUD

CHELSEA pulled off a major coup when they signed one of Europe's most popular soccer stars. He is one of the mega names in world soccer. He is, of course, the one and only RUUD GULLIT.

THINGS WORTH KNOWING ABOUT GULLIT:

● He was born in Surinam on September 1st, 1962.

● He began his professional career in 1978 with FA Haarlem. He scored 32 goals in 91 games.

● Because of his Dutch mother, he is able to play for Holland andin 1981 he gained his first cap, coming on as substitute for Frank Rijkaard in a win over Switzerland.

● Johan Cruyff was impressed by Ruud's talent and signed him in 1982 for Feyenoord.

● In 1984, Feyenoord won the Dutch League and Cup double.

● Ruud's fame spread throughout Europe. In 1985 PSV Eindhoven signed him and in the following two years he twice led them to the League championship, scoring 48 goals in 68 matches.

● In 1987, he was named European Footballer of the Year and Italy could resist him no longer. AC Milan handed over £5.7 million to sign him.

● One of his greatest moments came in 1988 when he inspired Holland to the European championship.

● The honours kept coming and, in 1989, having recovered from a severe knee injury, Gullit scored a sensational goal in the European Cup Final to help his side take the trophy with a 4-0 win over Steau Bucharest.

● In the summer of 1993 Sampdoria bought him for £5 million. He looked a new player and seemed to have put behind him his injuries and off-the-field disagreements. He later returned to Milan for a while before returning to Sampdoria.

● As a gesture of goodwill, Sampdoria gave him a free transfer in the summer of 1995. There was a queue of clubs, including megabucks offers from Japan. But he has always liked England and has great respect for Glen Hoddle. So, he chose Chelsea.

● Arsenal could have signed him as a teenager. Haarlem offered him at £80,000 but The Gunners turned him down.

● His dad was a Surinam soccer international.

● He is married with two daughters.

● He loves music, especially reggae and plays guitar and sings. He has had his own band and made successful recordings. His hero is Bob Marley.

● Don't expect him to become a top manager - he is more interested in television and has an active interest in politics.

HOW HE SEES HIMSELF:

"I think I have a few good years left yet. I have had my problems with injuries but that is behind me now and I feel as good as new. It is for others to decide if I am the same player as I was but I know how I feel - and I feel good."

ON CHELSEA:

"I have always admired English football and English footballers. I see this as a wonderful opportunity to play in what is probably the best League in the world. I have fulfilled an ambition by coming to England and what better club than to Chelsea where the manager is one of the best players of all time and there is such a progressive attitude."

GULLITT

"He is one of the outstanding players of our time and has had a marvellous career. He hasn't finished yet either."
JOHAN CRUYFF

"Ruud is one of the most exciting players of the last few decades. The Chelsea fans deserve the best and I want top players in my side. That's why we are always interested in players like him."
GLENN HODDLE

"A wonderul player, very skilful, very clever and great to watch. Ruud is a real entertainer."
DIEGO MARADONA

ENGLAND

SHOOT

David Platt

Who'd be a boss?

WHO'D BE a manager? Some stay happily in their jobs for years but most last two or three seasons or, in many cases, even less. It's a hard life...as we discovered.

Southampton boss Alan Ball once put things in a nutshell by saying: "Your first day in a new job as manager is a day nearer getting the sack." That's too true to be funny for some managers.

In January 1991, DAVE BOOTH parted company with Peterborough where he had been the boss for just 63 days. It is difficult to see what could be achieved in just nine weeks but there have been even shorter terms than Dave's.

Graham Taylor looks set to stay in charge at Wolves for some time but the club had two very short-term managers in the past. In November 1985 BILLY McGARRY left after only 61 days and a year later, in October 1986, BRIAN LITTLE also left Wolves after only 49 days as boss.

When JOHN TOSHACK gave up the job as manager of Wales after just one game he had been in charge for only 48 days, but the greatest casualty list is still at club level. At the start of last season BILLY BONDS of West Ham, STEVE WICKS of Scarborough, PHIL HENSON of Rotherham and KENNY SWAIN of Wigan were all early casualties and that does not seem uncommon. Clubs often seem to hit the panic button early in the season and change bosses.

The 1992-93 season was only 12 days old when PETER REID parted company with Manchester City and that has happened quite often.

Constant changes of managers is also a problem. During the 1994-95 season, Notts County had FOUR managers. The season began with MICK WALKER in charge; he was replaced in October by RUSSELL SLADE, who was then himself replaced by HOWARD KENDALL. Before Kendall could make his presence felt he was on his way and WAYNE JONES was left to look after things for the remainder of the season. Needless to say, County were relegated.

LEEDS have a remarkable record in that two of the biggest names in soccer were managers at Elland Road for very short terms. In September 1974, BRIAN CLOUGH left after just 44 days and history repeated itself a few years later when JOCK STEIN left in October 1978, also after exactly 44 days in charge.

But those big name casualties are not record holders. Jimmy McIlroy left Bolton in November 1970 after a 16 day reign; John Cochrane of Reading fared even worse back in April 1939 when he lasted 13 days; and more remarkably, Tim Ward was manager of Exeter for exactly one week. He left in March 1953 exactly SEVEN DAYS after starting.

But the shortest career in soccer management with a British club is that of Bill Lambton.

He was appointed manager of Scunthorpe on April 21st 1959. On April 23rd his side played Liverpool at Anfield and lost 3-0. On the way home Bill was sacked after just THREE DAYS in charge.

The moral of the story? **Don't be a manger!**

HOWARD KENDALL **OUT!**

JOCK STEIN **OUT!**

BRIAN CLOUGH **OUT!**

JOHN TOSHACK **OUT!**

SAD

Like it or not...club mascots are here to stay!

CUDDLY is not exactly the term you would use to describe your average footballer but some of the club mascots will either make you go 'ahhhh' and want to throw your arms around them...

...or make you go 'ughhhh' and make you want to throw up. The choice is yours.

Mascots are not new. In the immediate post World War II days many clubs paraded their mascots before the game, a practice that

fizzled out in the 60s as the mascots became more of a coconut shy on legs as 'fans' pelted the unfortunate mascots with just about anything they could lay their hands on.

Leyton Orient used to have a bloke walking round the pitch perimeter dressed as a Chinaman, complete with Aladdin's lamp. Eventually even the genie gave up as the

danger to life and limb took the fun out of it. In any case, three wishes wouldn't be enough to save Orient.

But in the last few seasons mascots have come back with a vengeance.

Fred The Red sounds a bit like a commie union leader but is in fact the mascot of Manchester United. Not only does Fred put in appearances at Old Trafford but has a whole range of designer merchandise in his honour.

Wolfie Wolf is the highly original mascot of Wolves. He looks harmless enough - nice and cuddly, floppy ears, wide eyes and all the rest but there's something about his grin. He's the sort of character that would make Red Riding Hood look like Jean-Claude Van Damme.

Hillsborough is the place to be for a really nice mascot, the sort you could take home to met mum. Ozzie the Owl is a giant cuddly toy. He is great on the wing and specialises in 'night games'! Despite their suspect form last season, wednesday must be one of the few clubs in the

country to give their crowd the bird.

Rammy the Ram does his best

OR MAD?

to look friendly at Derby County but with a Barry Horne stuck on each side of your head it's not easy to look like a big softie. Many of the Derby players have wanted to take on the role of Rammy The Ram but so far none have made the grade. Now if it were Alan SHEARER, it might be a different matter.

Sky Blue Sam has been sent to Coventry, just the treatment you would expect the rest of the herd to hand out to a blue elephant. Cuddly Sam - or should we be

friendly and call him Sky - happily skips round Highfield Road waving his huge feet to the fans - a bit like Dion Dublin really. Sky Blue Sam is nobody's fool though. He has a great memory and can even recall the last time Coventry won something.

In the late 70s Grimsby Town had an unusual mascot for a while. Her name was Sparky and she was a real, live chimpanzee from the local Cleethorpes Zoo. Sparky used to go to and sit through matches, nick the play-

ers clothes in the dressing room and generally create havoc everywhere she went.

In recent years, Cleethorpes Zoo has become Pleasure Island Theme Park, sponsors of Scunthorpe and suppliers of the Iron's mascot, a high bear called Billy Bob. Scunthorpe have campaigned for families to return to soccer for several seasons and Billy Bob has been doing his bit to bring a bit of fun to Glanford Stadium. The trouble is that the team's soccer has been a bit of white knuckle ride so the impact of Billy Bob hasn't been able to BEAR the full fruit.

And so we come to Birmingham City's brilliant invention. It is a sort of huge blue blob with two large nostrils. Just in case anyone is not sure what it is, it has been given a name - Blue Nose. Not the most popular of mascots, surely. In fact, it could be said that Birmingham invented Blue Nose and blew it!

But is he Sad...or Mad?

Identity Parade

JUMBLE BOOK

Unravel the letters to discover the name of this London club skipper.

SEWED IN SIN

SORT 'IM OUT

Re-arrange the letters to find a Northern star from the Midlands

CALM TRAP LONER

CHALLENGE MATCH:

The Mariners are followed by The Seagulls in the League table and behind them come The Seasiders with The Shrimpers in fourth place. Can you put them in the correct order of their real names?

WHAT DO YOU KNOW ABOUT...

....LIVERPOOL?

1. Which was the first European trophy Liverpool won?
A. European Cup; B. European Cup Winners Cup or C. UEFA Cup
2. Who was manager before Kenny Dalglish?
   A. Graeme Souness; B. Joe Fagan or C. Bob Paisley
3. Who has scored the most League goals for Liverpool in one season?
   A. Kenny Dalglish; B. Ian Rush or C. Roger Hunt
4. Kevin Keegan joined Liverpool from which club?
   A. Scunthorpe; B. Doncaster or C. Rotherham?
5. In the last ten years, Liverpool have been in four FA Cup Finals. Which of these teams was the one to beat them?
   A. Manchester United; B. Sunderland or C. Wimbledon

....CELTIC?

1. Who was manager at Parkhead before Lou Macari?
A. Liam Brady; B. David Hay or C. Bill McNeill
2. When Celtic won the European Cup, where was the Final played?
A. Wembley; B. Lisbon or C. Paris
3. Celtic's last title win was in 1987-88. Who finished second in that season?
   A. Rangers; B. Aberdeen or C. Hearts
4. Who was the last Celtic player to be named Scottish Footballer of the Year?
   A. Charlie Nicholas; B. John Collins or. C. Paul McStay
5. Which top English club manager starred as a player at Celtic? Was it -
   A. Bruce Rioch; B. Kenny Dalglish or C. Alex Ferguson

QUIZZES & PUZZLES

Can you name the star players in these various mini-puzzles?

ANSWERS PAGE 125

CLUE TRUE OR FALSE:

1. Rangers have won more Scottish League titles than Celtic.
2. Nottingham Forest and Aston Villa have jointly won the League Cup the most times.
3. Coventry are the only club to have played in every Division including the old Third Division North and South.
4. Lincoln City were the first club to suffer automatic relegation from the Football League.

HOW MANY YORKSHIRE SOCCER CLUBS CAN YOU NAME?

All the clues below have the names of soccer stars as their solutions. Enter the INITIALS of each name into the numbered segments of the ring, as directed by the figures in brackets. When the puzzle is completed, another famous football name will appear in the the ring, running clockwise, BUT NOT NECESSARILY STARTING AT No. 1. We've entered the first answer to start you off.

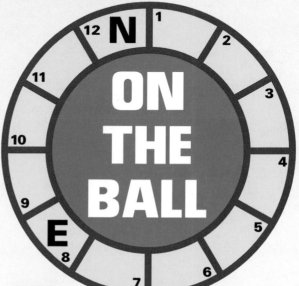

ON THE BALL

CLUES

A. Chelsea's former England Youth midfielder (8/12)
B. Former Argentine star who managed Spurs and Swindon (4/11)
C. Australian-born Leeds and England full-back (3/10)
D. Former Stamford Bridge striker at The Dell (9/7)
E. Villa's star Trinidad and Tobago striker (1/2)
F. Forest midfielder once of Man Utd and England (6/5)

WHAT DO YOU KNOW ABOUT: TONY COTTEE

1. Tony made his senior debut was for which London club?
A. Leyton Orient; B. West Ham or C. Millwall
2. On his debut for Everton he scored a hat-trick. Who was it against?
A. Newcastle; B. Blackburn or C. Manchester United
3. Tony's England debut was against which country in 1987?
A. Norway; B. Sweden or C. Denmark?

SHOOT

ASTON VILLA F.C.

PREPARED

ASTON VILLA

müller

Gary Charles

CHELSEA

Dennis Wise

WHO ARE the stars of tomorrow that you can see in action today? Every club has its up-and-coming heroes. A few years ago it was Ryan Giggs, Jamie Redknapp, Garry Flitcroft or Darren Anderton. Now there are others entering the scene so stand by for the next generation.

SIMON DONNELLY
Celtic

He has already been hailed as the new Dalglish and has the sort of talent that the fans believe will be the making of the future for The Bhoys. Simon has tremendous skill in shielding, shrugging off defenders and getting in a shot from a seemingly impossible situation. His 21st birthday is on December 1, 1995 but he has already come of age on the pitch.
"Simon is a great young player who has star written all over him. He has done ever so well in getting a first team place and keeping it. The fans think he is great - and they are right. He is the future of Celtic."
JOHN COLLINS

DAVID UNSWORTH
Everton

As Everton emerge from the gloom of recent seasons, David Unsworth is among the stars fighting for glory at Goodison. Born in Preston on October 16th, 1973, he had a great season last term and played his part in Everton's great FA Cup win. David also made his mark at England Under-21 level and it is only a matter of time before he wins a full cap.
"David has come through the youth scheme at the club and taken the chances that have presented themselves. He has not been at all out of place in the first team and I am sure that he is going to go on to be a big favourite at Goodison and win a lot of medals at the club."
DAVE WATSON

DAVID BECKHAM
Manchester United

Born in Leytonstone, David is one of a clutch of stars emerging at Old Trafford. There is so much talent coming through that it is frightening. David made his senior debut against Brighton in the Coca-Cola Cup two seasons ago and has been hovering around the first team ever since. He is still only 20 and looks certain for stardom during the next year or two.
"David has delivered every time he has played. It is not easy plunge into an established team now and then but he has done it and he will soon be a regular with a very big future."
STEVE BRUCE

THE NEXT

SPOTLIGHT ON THE STARS OF TOMORROW

GARRY KELLY
Leeds United

Leeds have also created an impressive youth set-up at Elland Road and they are reaping the benefits of it. One of their young stars has been around for a while and even played in the World Cup finals. Yet Gary Kelly is still only 21. He was born in Drogheda on July 9, 1974 and joined Leeds from the famous Home Farm Club. He is already a hero for club and country but still one to watch.

"Garry is still only a youngster but he is already so experienced. He is a great attacking full-back who is only going to get better. He is going to be a major star."
MARK BEENEY

GENERATION

JOHN HARTSON
Arsenal

Moving to Arsenal is a big step for anyone but when you are a youngster born in Swansea and given a soccer education at Luton, you might be forgiven for being overawed by the splendour of Highbury. Not John Hartson. He is still only 20 but plays like an old hand. Good news for Arsenal and also for Wales, where he is ready to step into some very well-known boots.

"John is an excellent player. He is not afraid to have a go and has done enough to show that he is the business. He can score goals and he can beat defenders. I'm sure he is going to become one of the big names in Arsenal history."
TONY ADAMS

STUART NETHERCOTT
Tottenham

Stuart emerged during last season when ex-Spurs boss Ossie Ardiles decided to give him the chance to show his paces. It worked and Stuart proved that he was worth his place as a regular member of both the Spurs squad and the England Under-21 squad.

Born on March 23, 1973 in Chadwell Heath, Stuart is a young lad who has made good and is getting better and better.

"He did very well last season and there is no doubt that he is going to feature more and more in the manager's plans. He is a good young defender with a brain, as well as physical abilities. He is going to be a star for sure."
GARY MABBUTT

RICHARD EDGHILL
Manchester City

Old Trafford is not the only grooming ground of the stars of the future. They have their goldmine at Maine Road as well. Richard Edghill has already made a name for himself in both the City first-team and in the England Under-21 side. Born in Oldham on September 23, 1974, Richard is one of the fastest defenders in the game and is certain to become a national hero.

"Richard has got what it takes to become a really big name. I have played against him in training and he is very strong and very quick. He shows great touches and it is difficult to remember that he is still a young lad. Definitely one to watch." NIALL QUINN

FUNNY OLD GAME!

NOBODY could accuse Newcastle of lacking enterprise - and not just on the pitch either. A few years ago they became the first club to launch their own brand of champagne. More recently they have gained another first by applying to be allowed to hold weddings at St. James's Park. Since their lounges are often booked for wedding receptions, The Magpies reckoned it would be a good idea to have the whole day at the famous ground, including the actual ceremony. If the law would allow it, The Magpies would even have weddings take place in the centre circle.

KEVIN KEEGAN is probably everyone's ideal soccer boss and was once everyone's ideal player. But 'Wor Kev' has had his moments of madness too. In August 1974 he was sent off twice in five days - in a friendly against Kaiserslautern and then in the FA Charity Shield match against Leeds at Wembley.

ON FEBRUARY 14th 1920, Ben Beynon lined up for Swansea against Queens Park Rangers. Nothing unusual about that perhaps except that only seven days earlier he had been played as a rugby international for Wales against Scotland.

IN SEPTEMBER 1915, a soldier of the London Irish Rifles led an attack on German trenches in Loos during the First World War. He led the way by kicking a football. That ball is still a museum piece at the Duke of York's Regiment museum in Chelsea.

ON December 6th 1952, Arsenal, Charlton, Chelsea, Brentford and Leyton Orient were all due to play home League fixtures but none of them did. It is the only case of London soccer being completely wiped out by fog.

CRAIG JOHNSTON, the former Liverpool star who invented the Predator boot, played for England's Under-21 side but was one of the most mixed-up players in the game. He was born in South Africa, brought up in Australia, had a Scottish grandfather and Irish grandmother. He is registered as a British citizen.

SOCCER shirts got more and more colourful but they'll probably never match the kit worn by Chesterfield for the 1890-91 season. The Spireites wore Union Jack shirts! Their performances never flagged!

SIR STANLEY MATTHEWS - one of the greatest footballers ever - celebrated his 80th birthday earlier this year. Sir Stan was the very first winner of the Footballer Of The Year award in 1948. He was playing for Blackpool at the time. Amazingly, he won it again when he was with Stoke - 15 years later

WHEN Raith Rovers won the Scottish Coca-Cola Cup, their video "Dancing On the Streets of Raith" turned into a major seller. After selling their first 10,000, Raith realised that they were also in with a chance of the Tennants Scottish Cup and the First Division Championship and began planning two sequels to their video hit.

Is it only a matter of time before "Dancing On The Streets Of Raith" I and II are in demand?

ALAN SHEARER believes he is not worth the £3.3 million that Blackburn paid for him when they signed him from Southampton. The modest maestro said: "Doctors, nurses and firemen - people who save lives - are the ones who are worth that sort of money, not footballers. We are just not worth all the money that is spent on transfers."

TOTTENHAM

For the Record

Record League victory:
9-0 v Bristol Rovers, Division Two, October 22, 1977

Record Cup victory:
13-2 v Crewe, FA Cup 4th Round (replay), February 3, 1960

Record defeat:
0-7 v Liverpool, Division One, September 2, 1978

Record attendance:
75,038 v Sunderland, FA Cup 6th Round, March 5, 1938

Most League points (2 for a win): 70, Division Two, 1919-20

Most League points (3 for a win): 77, Division One, 1984-85

Most League goals:
115, Division One, 1960-61

Highest League scorer in season:
Jimmy Greaves, 37, Division One, 1962-63

Most League goals in total aggregate:
Jimmy Greaves, 220, 1961-70

Most Capped player:
Pat Jennings, 74 (119), Northern Ireland

Most League appearances:
Steve Perryman, 655, 1969-86

Record Transfer Fee received:
£5,500,000 from Lazio for Paul Gascoigne, May 1992

Record Transfer Fee paid:
£2,800,000 to PSV Eindhoven for Gica Popescu, August 1994

Tottenham Hotspur are one of the most glamourous clubs in English football.

They always have been and always be, but their style hasn't always been matched by success on the field.

It is 35 years since they were last crowned Champions of England, far too long for a club of their stature.

It is remarkable when you consider some of the players that have worn the famous white shirt down the years. But despite the presence of the likes of Greaves, Hoddle, Ardiles, Gascoigne and Klinsmann, the League title has continued to elude them.

While their great North London rivals Arsenal have won two titles in the past six years, Spurs fans have had to be content with one FA Cup triumph in that time.

That came against Nottingham Forest in 1991, a record eighth victory in the oldest knock-out competition in the world.

But there is little doubt that Spurs fans would swap a couple of those victories for another League title.

And if Alan Sugar can continue to come up with the cash for new signings, and he can continue to persuade manager Gerry Francis to stay, then that title might not be too far away.

Continued over...

CLUB FOCUS No.6

TOTTENHAM HOTSPUR

Top Ten Transfers

PLAYER	FROM
Gary Lineker	Barcelona
Jimmy Greaves	Chelsea
Paul Gascoigne	Newcastle
Chris Waddle	Newcastle
Darren Anderton	Portsmouth
Jurgen Klinsmann	Monaco
Alan Gilzean	Dundee
Dave Mackay	Hearts
Pat Jennings	Watford
Ossie Ardiles	Huracan

Top Ten Managers

Bill Nicholson	1958-74
Arthur Rowe	1949-50
Terry Venables	1987-91
Ossie Ardiles	1993-94
Gerry Francis	1994-
Keith Burkinshaw	1976-84
David Pleat	1986-87
Peter Shreeves	1984-86, 1991-92
Terry Neill	1974-76
Peter McWilliam	1912-27

Top Ten Strikers

Jimmy Greaves	1961-69
Gary Lineker	1989-92
Jurgen Klinsmann	1994-95
Martin Peters	1969-74
Alan Gilzean	1964-73
Teddy Sheringham	1992-
Steve Archibald	1980-83
Chris Waddle	1985-89
Clive Allen	1984-88
Martin Chivers	1967-75

Roll of Honour

Division One Champions:
1950-51, 1960-61;
Division Two Champions
1919-20, 1949-50;
FA Cup Winners
1901, 1921, 1961, 1962, 1967, 1981, 1982, 1991;
League Cup Winners
1970-71, 1972-73.
European Cup-Winners' Cup Winners
1962-63;
UEFA Cup Winners
1971-72, 1983-84

Premiership Record 1994-95

Aug 20	SHEFF WED	(a)	W4-3
Aug 24	EVERTON	(h)	W2-1
Aug 27	MAN UTD	(h)	L0-1
Aug 30	IPSWICH	(a)	W3-1
Sep 12	SOUTHAMPTON	(h)	L1-2
Sep 17	LEICESTER	(a)	L1-3
Sep 24	NOTTM FOR	(h)	L1-4
Oct 01	WIMBLEDON	(a)	W2-1
Oct 08	QPR	(h)	D1-1
Oct 15	LEEDS	(a)	D1-1
Oct 22	MAN CITY	(a)	L2-5
Oct 29	WEST HAM	(h)	W3-1
Nov 05	BLACKBURN	(a)	L0-2
Nov 19	ASTON VILLA	(h)	L3-4
Nov 23	CHELSEA	(h)	D0-0
Nov 26	LIVERPOOL	(a)	D1-1
Dec 03	NEWCASTLE	(h)	W4-2
Dec 10	SHEFF WED	(h)	W3-1
Dec 17	EVERTON	(a)	D0-0
Dec 26	NORWICH	(a)	W2-0
Dec 27	C.PALACE	(h)	D0-0
Dec 31	COVENTRY	(a)	W4-0
Jan 02	ARSENAL	(h)	W1-0
Jan 14	WEST HAM	(a)	W2-1
Jan 25	ASTON VILLA	(a)	L0-1
Feb 05	BLACKBURN	(h)	W3-1
Feb 11	CHELSEA	(a)	D1-1
Feb 25	WIMBLEDON	(h)	L1-2
Mar 04	NOTTM FOR	(a)	D2-2
Mar 08	IPSWICH	(h)	W3-0
Mar 15	MAN UTD	(a)	D0-0
Mar 18	LEICESTER	(h)	W1-0
Mar 22	LIVERPOOL	(h)	D0-0
Apr 02	SOUTHAMPTON	(a)	L3-4
Apr 11	MAN CITY	(h)	W2-1
Apr 14	C.PALACE	(a)	D1-1
Apr 17	NORWICH	(h)	W1-0
Apr 29	ARSENAL	(a)	D1-1
May 03	NEWCASTLE	(a)	D3-3
May 06	QPR	(a)	L1-2
May 09	COVENTRY	(h)	L1-3
May 14	LEEDS	(h)	D1-1

Top League Scorers 1994-95

Klinsmann	20
Sheringham	18
Barmby	9
Anderton	5
Dumitrescu	4
Popescu	3
Calderwood	2

Flowers Power

The story so far

Born in Kenilworth on February 3rd 1967, Tim began his soccer career as soon as he left school by joining Wolves as an apprentice. His boss in those days was Tommy Docherty, one of the greatest characters the game has ever known. Tim's boyhood hero was Ray Clemence and he hoped that one day he might follow in Ray's famous footsteps and play for England.

Tim made his first-team debut on August 25th, 1984 when Wolves drew 2-2 with Sheffield United. After two seasons in the first-team squad Tim had a loan spell with Southampton which became a permanent move when he signed on June 13th 1986, Wolves receiving £70,000. During the next couple of seasons, Flowers twice had loan spells with Swindon but eventually he made The Saint's

No.1 jersey his own. Eventually, of course, his performances were so good so often that Kenny Dalglish could not resist signing him in November 1993 for a record £2 million.

SOCCER life is not always a bed of roses - not even if your name is Tim Flowers. But ask any good 'keeper and he'll tell you that you have to take the knocks along with the bouquets. Blackburn's England goalkeeper has suffered a few downs in the past, but is definitely on the way up with the League Champions.

Tim's top of the stoppers

Your country needs you!

While learning his trade at Wolves, Tim made the England youth team. But there was more to come since he later added to those caps when he was picked to play for the Under-21 side, his first game being against Morocco on June 7th 1987. He kept a clean sheet as England won 2-0 and he was called up for another two appearances before becoming over age. Finally he achieved his ambition of a full England cap when he lined up against Brazil in Washington, USA on June 13th, 1993. It was a 1-1 draw and Tim became a regular part of the England senior set-up after that.

Tim's trophies

Tim's big ambitions now are to win medals and awards. He desperately wants to help Blackburn win the European Cup but would settle for a collection of all the domestic honours English football can offer. In 1993 he was named Southampton's Player of the Year and you can't help feeling that he has a lot more similar awards to come in the future.

Flowers Future

"I am still only 28, which is young for a goalkeeper, and I feel that I am still learning. I know that I am England No. 2 behind David Seaman and perhaps I will be for some time to come. I just have to be patient and wait my chance. My club future is with Blackburn and I wouldn't want to be anywhere else. We are a young side with a big future and I want to be part of it."

SCOTLAND

Colin Hendry

SING WHEN WE'RE WINNIN'

But who was on song in '96?

Blackburn
Premiership Champions

Everton
FA Cup Winners

Ajax
European Cup Winners

Liverpool
Coca-Cola Cup Winners

Alan Shearer and Blackburn were the toast of English football at the end of one of the most fascinating seasons for years.

England striker Shearer had more reasons to celebrate than most after picking up a unique hat-trick of top honours.

In addition to winning a Championship medal, Shearer's 34 goals made him the proud owner of the coveted Golden Shoe - and he was also voted by his fellow pros as the Player of the Year.

The 1994-95 season will definitely go down as Shearer's Season, but it's time to pay tribute to all the big-name winners of some of the most prestigious awards at home and abroad.

Welcome to the SHOOT ANNUAL roll of honour...

CHAMPIONS!

Spot On: Shearer scores a penalty against Leeds

Tim to Party: Sherwood gets to grips with the trophy

Sutton Pretty: Chris scores against QPR

SHOOT salutes the Pride of the Premiers

Mark of Class: Hateley celebrates another title

We are No.1: Mark Atkins points Rovers to the top

King Richard: Gough holds the trophy aloft... ...again

Moore the Merrier: Craig nets against Partick

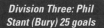
Division Three: Phil
Stant (Bury) 25 goals

Division
Two: Gary
Bennett
(Wrexham)
29 goals

Scottish Premier
Division: Tommy Coyne
(Motherwell) 16 goals

Golden Wonders

Goalscorers are football's glory boys, the most valuable players in the game. And they don't come any better than these guys...last season's SHOOT/adidas Golden Shoe winners...

Cor, thanks boss, it's just what I've always wanted!

Division One:
John Aldridge
(Tranmere)
24 goals

Premiership:
Alan Shearer
(Blackburn)
34 goals

Ronny Rosenthal won the award for Best Performance in the FA Cup - and the added bonus of having it presented by Sam Fox

Jurgen Klinsmann was voted Best Overseas Player - and promptly went back overseas!

Saint Matt picked up the Player of the Year award and the Goal of the Season award, but he had to get his from Terry Christian!

Forget the Oscars, forget the Brits, the biggest awards night of 1995 took place at London's Planet Hollywood. It was the first ever IPC Football Group Awards and what a night it was. Here are just a few of the winners on a night of a thousand stars...

And the

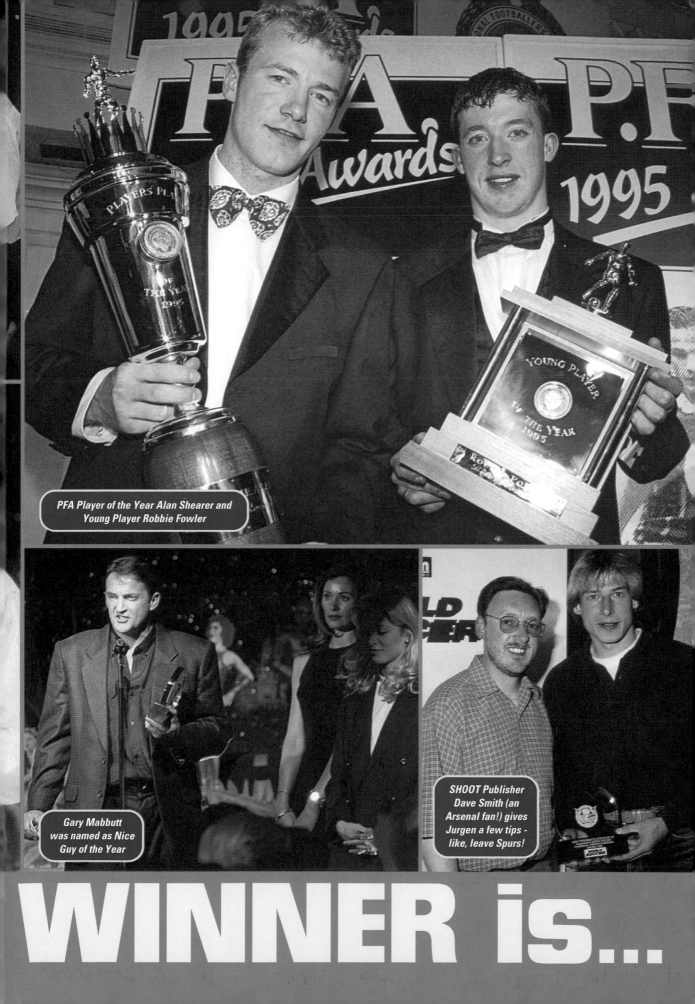

PFA Player of the Year Alan Shearer and Young Player Robbie Fowler

Gary Mabbutt was named as Nice Guy of the Year

SHOOT Publisher Dave Smith (an Arsenal fan!) gives Jurgen a few tips - like, leave Spurs!

WINNER is...

'WE'RE GOING

Picture tribute to the Endsleigh climbers

After a long hard season, seven teams were celebrating promotion last summer . They'd toiled and sweated to achieve their ultimate goal, be it automatically or via the Play-Offs. SHOOT pays tribute to the Magnificent Seven...

Division One Champions: Middlesbrough

Division One Play-Offs: Bolton

UP...'

Division Two Champions: Birmingham

Division Two Play-Offs: Huddersfield

STONE'S PAINTS Coca-Cola UMBRO

Division Three Champions: Carlisle

Division Three Play-Offs: Chesterfield

Division Three Promoted: Walsall

European Cup: Ajax

EUROCRATS!

UEFA °
Cup:
Parma

Cup-Winners'
Cup :
Real Zaragoza

Spotlight on the Champions of Europe

CUP CRAZY!

Scottish Cup Winners: Celtic

Coca-Cola Cup Winners: Liverpool

Scottish Coca Cola Cup Winners: Raith Rovers

We salute the Cup kings

HOW WELL DID YOU DO? QUIZ AND PUZZLE ANSWERS

IDENTITY PARADE (Pages 40-41)

CAPITAL MOVES
A. Andy Impey plays for QPR (E), B. Martin Allen plays for West Ham (C), C. John Spencer plays for Chelsea (B), D. Justin Edinburgh plays for Spurs (F), E. Robbie Earle plays for Wimbledon (A), F. Nigel Winterburn plays for Arsenal (D).

What do you about... MAN. UNITED?
1.B; 2.B; 3.C; 4.A; 5.B.

What do you know about...RANGERS
1.A; 2.A; 3.C; 4.A; 5.C.

PREMIERSHIP SKIPPER
Steve Bruce

STAR RIDDLE
Mark Hateley

GIVE US A CLUE
Peter Beardsley

STAR TRAIL
Tim Flowers

TAKE A LETTER
Wolves; Ron; I's Gee-gee; Hoddle; Tea. - W.R.I.G.H.T.

I'LL NAME THAT STAR
1. Dave Seaman; 2. David Burrows; 3. Chris Waddle; 4. Roy Keane; 5. Henning Berg.

TYNESIDE TEASER
Ruel Fox

CAPITAL GOLD
Justin Edinburgh

TONY YEBOAH
1. Eintracht Frankfut, 2. Ghana, 3. Ipswich Town.

CROSSWORD (Page 46)
ACROSS 1. Stan Collymore, 8. Hoddle, 9. Colombia, 10. Earl, 11. Hislop, 12+14D PSV Eindhoven, 13. Crewe Alexandra, 17. Underhill, 18. Little, 20. Hansen, 21. Stoichkov, 24. Ince, 25. Hill, 26. Alf, 27. Links, 28. Karl.

DOWN 1.Schmeichel, 2. Anderlecht, 3. Overhead, 4. Lucas, 5. Moldova, 7. Hibs, 12. Parkinson, 15. Norway, 16. Blundell, 19. Trials, 22. Tait, 23. Hull, 24. IFK, 26+6D. AS Roma.

WORDSEARCH (Page 47)

IDENTITY PARADE (Pages 100-101)

CHALLENGE MATCH:
1. Grimsby Town, 2. Brighton, 3. Blackpool, 4. Southend.

TONY COTTEE
1.B; 2.A; 3.B.

CLUB TRUE OR FALSE:
A: 1. True; 2. False; 3. True; 4. True.

ON THE BALL
A. Eddie Newton, B. Osie Ardilles, C. Tony Dorigo, D. Neil Shipperley, E. Dwight Yorke, F. Neil Webb. Name on the ball — Andy Townsend (It starts at No.11).

YORKSHIRE CLUBS
Leeds, Sheffield Wed, Sheffield Utd, Barnsley, Bradford City, Huddersfield, Rotherham, York, Doncaster, Scarborough.

What do you know about...LIVERPOOL?
1.C; 2.B; 3.C; 4.A; 5.C.

What do you know about...CELTIC?
1.A; 2.B; 3.C; 4.C; 5.B.

SORT 'IM OUT
Carlton Palmer

JUMBLE BOOK
Dennis Wise

in England and Scotland

Champions

SCOTTISH

RANGERS

MULTI METALS

McEWAN'S LAGER

McEWAN'S LAGER

ISBN 1-85277-087-2